ESSENTIAL CHEMISTRY

CHEMICAL
BONDS

ESSENTIAL CHEMISTRY

ESSENTIAL CHEMISTRY

CHEMICAL BONDS

PHILLIP MANNING

CHELSEA HOUSE
PUBLISHERS
An imprint of Infobase Publishing

CHEMICAL BONDS

Chelsea House
An imprint of Infobase Publishing
132 West 31st Street
New York NY 10001

Library of Congress Cataloging-in-Publication Data

Manning, Phillip, 1936-
 Chemical bonds / Phillip Manning.
    p. cm. — (Essential chemistry)
 Includes bibliographical references and index.
 ISBN 978-0-7910-9740-3 (hardcover)
 1. Chemical bonds. I. Title. II. Series.

 QD461.M25 2008
 541'.224—dc22   2008001981

Chelsea House books are available at special discounts when purchased in bulk quantities for businesses, associations, institutions, or sales promotions. Please call our Special Sales Department in New York at (212) 967-8800 or (800) 322-8755.

You can find Chelsea House on the World Wide Web at http://www.chelseahouse.com

Text design by Erik Lindstrom
Cover design by Ben Peterson

Printed in the United States of America

Bang NMSG 10 9 8 7 6 5 4 3 2 1

This book is printed on acid-free paper.

All links and Web addresses were checked and verified to be correct at the time of publication. Because of the dynamic nature of the Web, some addresses and links may have changed since publication and may no longer be valid.

CONTENTS

Stardust

Modern life requires a mind-boggling array of materials, some natural but many man-made. A simple drinking cup, for example, might be made of Styrofoam or paper or glass. Consumers can choose the container that fits their needs at the moment— Styrofoam for hot coffee, paper for a sip of water at the gym, glass for a soft drink on the porch. Home storage cabinets can be made of **metals** or wood or plastic. Space shuttles are assembled from silicon and steel—and hundreds of other materials. All of these items owe their properties to the **chemical bonds** between the **atoms** that make up the substance.

Why do sodium atoms link together to form a silvery metal that reacts violently with water? What makes an atom of chlorine, a slightly heavier **element**, bond with another chlorine atom to form a poisonous gas that does not react with water at all? Furthermore, why does the combination of sodium and chlorine produce the white, crystalline substance called table salt, which does not react with water and is not, thank goodness, lethal? The nature of these substances is determined by their chemical bonds. The nature of these bonds is determined by the atoms. And, believe it or not, the nature of the atoms is determined by the stars.

MADE BY THE STARS

Almost everything in our lives—from paper cups to space shuttles, including Earth itself and every creature on it—is made of stardust. "Made of stardust" is not some overblown figure of speech. It is literally true. Scientists began to figure out the origins of atoms in the 1940s during a long-running debate about the nature of the cosmos itself: Was the **big bang theory** of an expanding universe true or was the **steady state theory** of a universe with no beginning or end correct?

The fun-loving physicist George Gamow led the big bang contingent; the English astronomer Fred Hoyle championed the steady state theory. The big bang theory correctly predicted that the visible universe is composed of 90% hydrogen atoms and 9% helium atoms with all the other elements making up only 1% of the total. Unfortunately, the big bang theory could not explain the origin of that crucial 1%, the part of the universe made up of the heavier elements, such as oxygen, carbon, and iron.

Despite Gamow's inability to account for the origin of the heavy elements, the big bang theory would eventually win out over the steady state concept. The discovery in the 1960s of **cosmic microwave background radiation** was a predicted result of the big bang, but the steady state theory could not account for it. The steady state theory was headed for the forgotten-theory trash can, but its principal advocate had a new big idea that answered the biggest problem associated with the big bang: If the heavy elements were not formed in the big bang, where did they come from?

GEORGE GAMOW
(1904–1968)

The life of George Gamow (pronounced Gam-off) reads like a mix of suspense fiction and fairy tale. Blond, six-foot-three-inches tall, with milk-bottle thick glasses, he combined brilliant thinking with clever jokes and a clear, humorous style of writing about science for the public.

Gamow was born in the part of the Russian Empire known today as Ukraine. He studied with the best physicists of his day in Göttingen, Copenhagen, and Cambridge. At Copenhagen, he enjoyed American Western movies, once challenging Niels Bohr to a gun fight. There is no record of who won, but Bohr was likely drenched by Gamow's water pistol.

As the Communist government began to oppress intellectuals, Gamow tried to escape the Soviet Union. He first tried rowing across the Black Sea to Turkey, a distance of about 170 miles (273 kilometers), accompanied by his wife, a little food, and two bottles of brandy. Not too surprisingly, this attempt did not succeed. He finally managed to get out of the Soviet Union in 1933 by defecting after attending a scientific conference in Brussels. He settled in the United States a short time later.

Gamow could combine serious science with a less than serious presentation. This is clear not only in his wonderful books of popular science but also in a famous paper titled "The Origin of the Chemical Elements." With coauthor Ralph Alpher, Gamow argued for the big bang theory and attempted to show how the big bang created the elements. The paper was a landmark in that it correctly predicted the amounts of hydrogen, helium, and the heavier elements in the universe. Its flaw was that the authors also tried to show that all the

continues

continued

elements were created during the big bang, a conclusion that proved false.

Still, the paper was crucially important in the development of modern cosmology. But Gamow could not resist adding a twist to it. To him, the name Alpher sounded like alpha, the first letter of the Greek alphabet. Gamow, of course, sounds like gamma, the third Greek letter. So, to fill in the gap, Gamow added the name of his friend, the famous physicist Hans Bethe, as a coauthor. The result was the Alpher-Bethe-Gamow theory, usually referred to as the Alpha-Beta-Gamma theory.

Figure 1.1   Cosmology pioneer George Gamow

In 1957, Fred Hoyle showed how the heavier elements could be forged by nuclear reactions in the stars. According to Hoyle, these elements are created when the extreme temperatures of the stars fuse together the **nuclei** of lighter elements. Physicists soon proposed a series of nuclear reactions that accounted for the formation of all the elements. The early universe, cosmologists now believe, formed with a big bang that produced hydrogen and helium. Later, the hydrogen and helium clumped together to form stars, which carried out reactions to form heavier elements. And the birth and death of billions of stars created the heavier atoms that can bond with one another to form planets like Earth and all the materials we use every day.

EINSTEIN'S DISCOVERY

Over 2,000 years ago, Greek philosophers were debating the existence of atoms. Could substances be forever subdivided or was there some irreducible structure that gave matter its unique properties? What made iron hard and heavy at room temperature while oxygen was light and airy? Although John Dalton had published a theory of atoms early in the nineteenth century and Dmitri Mendeleyev had based his **periodic table** of the elements on atoms in 1869, doubts about their existence lingered. These uncertainties were not completely resolved until the early twentieth century when a brash young Swiss patent clerk named Albert Einstein decided to address the problem of **Brownian motion**.

Robert Brown was a Scottish botanist and an accomplished microscopist. In 1827, he suspended grains of pollen in water and, watching them through his microscope, found that "they were very evidently in motion." The motion he observed was a random jiggling of the pollen. He satisfied himself that the movement of the grains was not due to currents or eddies in the water, but he was unable to determine what caused the motion.

No one else could explain it either, and so matters stood until 1905 when Einstein published a paper that cleared up the mystery of the jiggling pollen grains. His first sentence got right to the heart of the matter: "In this paper," Einstein wrote, "it will be shown that, according to the molecular-kinetic theory of heat, bodies of a microscopically visible size suspended in liquids must, as a result of thermal molecular motions, perform motions of such magnitudes that they can be easily observed with a microscope." In other words, the random movement of water **molecules** bumping against the pollen grains caused

Brownian motion. Therefore, molecules—and, by inference, atoms—must exist. For anyone else, this paper would have been a career highlight. But for Einstein, it was just the beginning. In that same year, he published two other papers that were at least as important. One of them toppled the wave theory of light that had prevailed for a century. The other proposed the special theory of relativity, which led to the best known equation in the world, $E = mc^2$.

After the publication of Einstein's paper on Brownian motion, scientists knew that atoms and molecules existed. But what did they look like? Were they hard, uniform balls, like tiny marbles? Or did atoms have an internal structure of their own?

One of the first scientists to investigate the makeup of atoms was a New Zealand country boy, a brilliant physicist named Ernest Rutherford. Rutherford did much of his early work in Canada and in Manchester, England, before becoming director of the famous Cavendish Laboratory in Cambridge, England. His early research on **radioactive elements** led him to conclude that their emissions came in two forms. Rutherford named them **alpha** and **beta particles** after the first two letters of the Greek alphabet. As he began exploring the nature of atoms, Rutherford decided to see what happened to alpha particles when they were fired at a thin sheet of gold foil.

From previous experiments, Rutherford knew that alpha particles were much bigger than **electrons** (which had been identified earlier as tiny, negatively charged particles by the Nobel Prize–winning physicist J.J. Thomson, Rutherford's mentor in graduate school and his predecessor at the Cavendish). He also knew that alpha particles carry a positive charge. He began studying the alpha particles further using a simple apparatus: a source of alpha particles, a sheet of gold foil, and a detection screen that glowed briefly whenever an alpha particle struck it. After many tedious experiments, Rutherford discovered that some of the alpha particles passed through the gold foil, and some had been deflected. A few had bounced directly back toward the source of the radiation. This was a surprising result. It was like shooting cannon balls at tissue paper and having some of them come back at you. Clearly, gold atoms contained something more massive than electrons, something that could make an alpha particle reverse direction upon impact.

Rutherford figured that the only way gold atoms could make the positively charged alpha particles bounce backward was if the gold atoms contained a small, dense mass carrying a positive charge. In a head-on collision, that charged mass would strongly repel an alpha particle. And because the atom's positive charge was concentrated in a small space, only a few of the bombarding particles would be repelled, while the rest would pass through. Finally, Rutherford announced his new structure of the atom. The atom, he said, was composed of a tiny positively charged nucleus with even tinier negatively charged electrons circling it. So small was the nucleus that if the atom was the size of a football stadium, the nucleus would only be the size of a marble. Atoms, it seems, are mostly empty space.

Rutherford published his structure of the atom in 1911. The new structure resembled the solar system. This arrangement was familiar to scientists and was quickly adopted by them. There was a problem, however. A negatively charged electron circling a positively charged nucleus should emit **electromagnetic radiation**, lose energy, and spiral down into the nucleus. According to the laws of physics known at the time, Rutherford's atom, made up of negatively charged particles in stable orbit around a positive center, was impossible. It could not exist.

THE GREAT LEAP FORWARD

A similarly vexing puzzle had bedeviled physicists a few years earlier. It was called the blackbody problem. A blackbody is a hypothetical object that absorbs all electromagnetic radiation that falls on it. Electromagnetic radiation is pure energy, waves that have no **mass**. Electromagnetic waves range from the highly energetic gamma and cosmic rays to low-energy radio waves. The rays in the visible part of the electromagnetic spectrum—those detectable by the human eye—are called light waves.

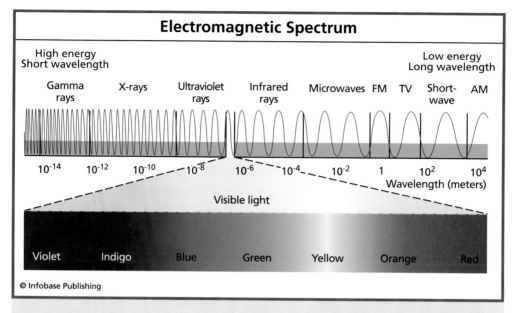

Figure 1.2　Colors are the waves in the electromagnetic spectrum that are visible to the human eye.

When heated, a blackbody radiates electromagnetic waves. Under some conditions, a blackbody isn't black at all. When the radiation emitted by a blackbody has wavelengths in the visible region of the electromagnetic spectrum, we see them as light.

Many common objects—a fireplace poker, for instance—mimic blackbodies. If you heat a poker, it stays the same color initially, but you can feel heat radiating from it in the form of infrared radiation. Radiation of this wavelength is invisible to our eyes but detectable by our hands—because your hand feels hot if you hold it close to the heated poker. Heat the poker to a higher temperature, and it begins to glow. It is now emitting more energetic waves. These waves are visible to us as the color red. Heat the poker even more and it turns white hot, because white is a mixture of all the colors in the visible spectrum, including the higher energy waves. Higher temperatures produce more energetic, higher-intensity radiation.

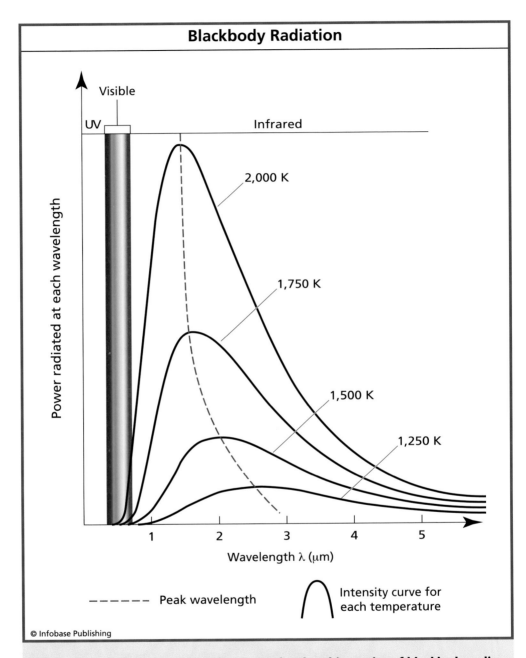

Figure 1.3 This graph shows the energy level and intensity of blackbody radiation. An increase in the temperature of a blackbody is accompanied by in increase in the energy level and intensity of the waves.

This characteristic blackbody spectrum holds for objects other than fireplace pokers. In fact, the spectrum of electromagnetic radiation emitted by any substance depends only on its temperature and is independent of the substance itself.

The characteristic spectrum of blackbodies was determined experimentally in the nineteenth century. But it could not be explained by the physics of Newton and Maxwell. (The great English scientist Isaac Newton formulated the laws of motion and gravity in 1687; James Clerk Maxwell, a Scottish physicist, published his laws of electricity and magnetism in 1871.)

The physics of Newton and Maxwell predicted that a heated body would emit an infinite amount of very high energy radiation.

This prediction was based on the notion that a blackbody is composed of tiny **oscillators** that produce a continuum of waves, like those you get when you pluck the strings of a violin. But the spectrum physicists predicted for blackbody radiation—an infinite amount of high-energy radiation—and the experimental data did not fit. They were not even close. And this was the problem that Max Planck was working on in 1900.

Planck was a brilliant German physicist with a button-down approach to his work. Although historians of science have studied extensively the breakthrough that led Planck to **quantum mechanics**, nobody can be sure exactly what was in his orderly, disciplined mind when he devised the equation that revolutionized physics. In any case, after examining many ideas, Planck finally tried the unthinkable: What if energy was not continuous? What if it came in tiny, discrete packets? He wrote down his equation.

$$E = nhf$$

In this equation, E is the energy of the oscillators in the blackbody, n is the number of oscillators, f is the frequency of oscillation, and h is a very small number. This number is known today as Planck's constant. It is usually represented using **scientific notation** as 6.6×10^{-34} joule-seconds. (A joule is the International System of Units (SI) unit of work. Abbreviated J, a joule is equal to 0.2388 calories.) In decimal form, Planck's constant looks like this:

$$0.00000000000000000000000000000000066$$

When Planck used his equation to calculate the spectrum of blackbody radiation, he came up with a result that agreed perfectly with experimental results. More importantly, he had discovered quantum mechanics, because this simple equation forms the basis of quantum theory. When applied to the physics of blackbodies, it implies that energy is not continuous but comes in tiny, irreducible packets, or **quanta** (a word coined by Planck himself), that are directly proportional to the frequency of an oscillator.

Planck presented his solution to the blackbody problem at the December 1900 meeting of the Berlin Physical Society. At the time, no one, probably not even Planck himself, grasped the implications of the simple equation he used to solve it. His equation was considered to be a nice mathematical trick but one with no particular physical significance. It was useful, but did not necessarily represent the way the blackbodies actually worked.

BOHR TO THE RESCUE

Niels Bohr was born with a scientific silver spoon in his mouth. He came from one of Denmark's prominent intellectual families. His sterling background helped him get a first-class education. After getting his college degree, he studied under J.J. Thomson in Cambridge. Then he went to work for Ernest Rutherford, one year after Rutherford had published the structure of his impossible atom, the atom that could not—but obviously did—exist. Bohr's burning desire was to discover what held the electrons in Rutherford's atom in place. What kept the negatively charged electrons from falling into the positively charged atomic nucleus?

Figure 1.4 Niels Bohr, father of the modern atom

Bohr knew of Max Planck's work with blackbodies, and he began to wonder: What if atoms exhibited the same quantum nature as blackbodies? What if the energies of electrons in an atom were not continuous but could assume only certain values?

After a year with Rutherford, Bohr returned home to Copenhagen to continue his work. But progress was slow until he began to study the spectrum of hydrogen. When hydrogen atoms are excited by an electrical discharge, they emit radiation. When the radiation passes through a prism, the emissions appear as sharp lines of specific wavelengths. After studying the emission lines, Bohr proposed a new structure for the hydrogen atom.

Like Rutherford, he pictured the atom as having a tiny nucleus with an electron circling it like a planet orbiting the Sun. But Bohr postulated that each electron can only have certain energies. Consider a hydrogen atom with one electron and two energy levels. (Hydrogen actually has more than two energy levels, but for simplicity's sake only two will be considered in this example.) An electron can jump from a lower energy level to a higher one by absorbing electromagnetic radiation in the form of a **photon**. Or it can go from a higher energy level to a lower one by ejecting a photon. But no intermediate energy levels exist. The atom is either

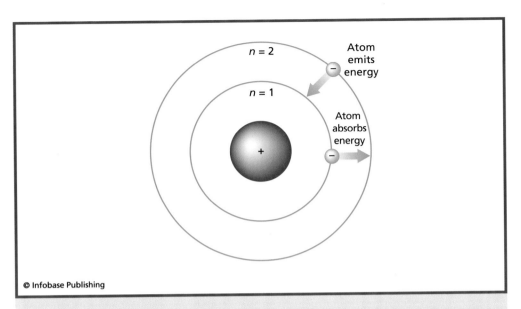

Figure 1.5 **An atom emits energy when an electron moves from a higher energy level to a lower energy level. When an atom absorbs energy, an electron moves from a lower energy level to a higher one.**

in one state or the other, and (with the loss or gain of energy) it transitions instantaneously between the two.

Bohr's application of Planck's ideas to Rutherford's atomic structure solved the impossible-atom problem. The energy of an electron in an atom was fixed. An atom could go from one energy state to another, but an electron could not emit a continuous stream of radiation and spiral into the nucleus. Quantum rules prohibit it.

With this model, it was now possible to calculate the energy difference between the orbits of an electron in a hydrogen atom using Planck's equation. In the example of the simplified hydrogen atom with one electron and two possible energy levels, the equation determining the frequency of the emitted radiation as the electron went from a higher energy state E_2 to a lower one E_1 would be

$$E_2 - E_1 = hf$$

where h is Planck's constant and f is the frequency of the emitted radiation.

Because hydrogen has more than two energy levels, it actually emits electromagnetic radiation at more than one frequency. Bohr's formulation accounted for all of hydrogen's observed emissions. Bohr published his new atomic structure in 1913. According to Albert Einstein, the Bohr model of the atom was "one of the greatest discoveries."

At first, Bohr confined his investigations to hydrogen. It is the simplest atom, consisting of a positively charged nucleus with one negatively charged electron circling it. But what about helium? Or sodium? Or any of the heavier elements? Bohr knew his theory of the atom had to be extended to other elements. To account for the properties of other atoms, Bohr borrowed a concept originally introduced by J.J. Thomson. The idea was that electrons in atoms occupy shells surrounding the nucleus. An atom can be thought of as an onion, with each layer of the onion representing one shell. Bohr extended Thomson's idea by assigning specific energies to each shell.

Using this concept, Bohr could build imaginary atoms electron by electron. After hydrogen came helium with two electrons. Helium is a very stable element, reluctant to lose or gain electrons. So, Bohr concluded that two electrons completely filled the first energy shell in an atom. Additional electrons would have to go into another shell. Bohr then determined that it took eight electrons to fill the next energy shell. Drawing on spectroscopic data, his knowledge of the periodic nature of the elements, and the natural intuitive genius that marked his entire career, Bohr extended his atomic theory to all the elements.

The Bohr atom went a long way toward explaining the nature of atoms. Still, there were problems. Scientists could calculate the wavelengths of the emission lines in the spectrum of hydrogen using the Bohr model, but the model could not account for the spectra of heavier atoms. However, the biggest problem with the

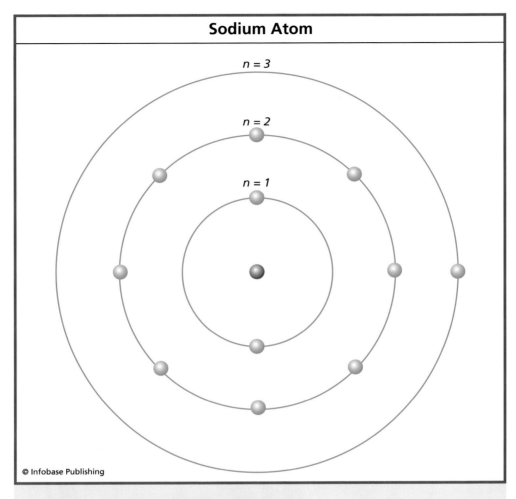

Sodium Atom

n = 3

n = 2

n = 1

© Infobase Publishing

Figure 1.6   The Bohr model of a sodium atom

Bohr atom lay in its arbitrary nature. The model accurately pre-dicted some experimental results, but it had no solid scientific footing. It explained nothing. What determines the energy levels of the electrons in a shell? Why are two electrons enough to fill the first energy shell in an atom, while eight electrons are required to fill the next one? While some scientists struggled to understand the laws that governed Bohr's atom, other scientists were working on a different problem. The problem was light. Was it a wave or a particle? That problem, when solved, would lead to a new structure that would replace Bohr's solar system model of the atom.

EINSTEIN AND THE NATURE OF LIGHT

More than 200 years ago, an Englishman named Thomas Young performed a set of experiments aimed at establishing the nature of light. The crucial one is known as the double slit experiment. In this experiment, light passes through a single slit (or pinhole) and continues on through a double slit. The result is a pattern of light and dark bands. This **interference pattern** is characteristic of waves and would be impossible to produce if light was a particle. Later, Maxwell's theory, which treated electromagnetic radiation as a wave, reinforced Young's results. So, by the beginning of the twentieth century, scientists were certain that light was a wave.

One exception was Albert Einstein. In 1905—the same year he published his work on Brownian motion—Einstein was trying to explain the **photoelectric effect**. The effect happens when electromagnetic radiation strikes a substance (usually a metal plate) and knocks electrons loose. When the radiation is of a single wavelength or color (monochromatic light) scientists observed experimental results that were hard to explain if light was a wave. For example, when the radiation source (the light) was moved closer to the metal, the intensity of the light (the number of waves striking the metal surface) increased. This meant more energy was hitting the metal plate. More energy should produce electrons with more energy. In fact, although more electrons were knocked out of the metal, the energy of the electrons stayed the same no matter how close to the metal plate the light was placed. The physics of the time could not explain this and other aspects of the photoelectric effect.

After working through Planck's calculations about the quantum nature of blackbody radiation, Einstein hypothesized that light might also be discontinuous. It might come in packets or quanta, like the electromagnetic radiation emitted by blackbodies. If light came in discrete packets, he reasoned, then making

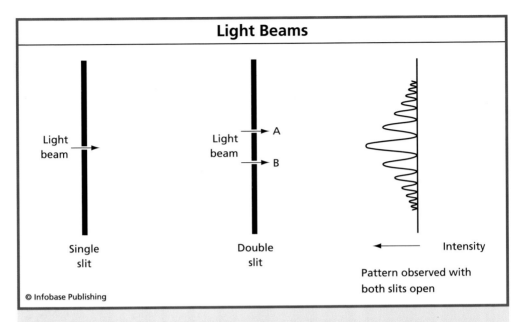

Light Beams

Light beam

Single slit

Light beam

A

B

Double slit

Intensity

Pattern observed with both slits open

© Infobase Publishing

Figure 1.7 In Young's double slit experiment, light passes through one slit and then into two slits. The patterns produced by the light proved that light travels as waves rather than particles.

the light brighter by moving the source closer to the metal would indeed knock more electrons out of the metal. But the energy of the packets (later named photons) would stay the same. Because the energy of the photons determines the energy of the ejected electrons, the energy of those electrons would not change. This was exactly the result scientists had obtained experimentally. Einstein had explained the photoelectric effect. He had also discovered the quantum (or particle) nature of light, reinforcing the ideas first proposed by Max Planck.

Still, the interference patterns from the double slit experiment clearly indicated that light was a wave. How could Einstein reconcile his conclusions about the particle nature of light with the results of the double slit experiment? Was it possible that light could act as either particle or wave?

Einstein was cautious about promoting this revolutionary idea. Furthermore, he was absorbed in sorting out another set of revolutionary ideas: the general theory of relativity. After clearing that up, though, Einstein returned to the problems of light and quantum mechanics and finally accepted the hard-to-accept solution: Light has a dual nature—sometimes it acts like a particle, sometimes it acts like a wave.

THE MODERN ATOM: STRANGER AND STRANGER

As physicists wrestled with the quandary posed by the dual nature of light, a young Frenchman named Louis de Broglie came up with an even bolder idea: If light could be both wave and particle, why could not electrons also display both of these properties? In fact, de Broglie hypothesized that all matter from electrons to volleyballs exhibits both wave and particle characteristics. But his equations showed that in larger bodies, bodies big enough to be seen by the human eye, the wave character was negligible. This is why a volleyball travels in a smooth trajectory over a net rather than moving in waves. But electrons are small enough that their wave characteristics play a large role in their behavior. De Broglie was unable to take his great insight further. That task would fall to a gifted Austrian physicist named Erwin Schrödinger.

Shortly after reading de Broglie's paper, Schrödinger developed an equation describing the wave behavior of electrons in an atom. The solutions to the wave equation produced the discrete energy levels hypothesized by Bohr. For the first time, physicists could rigorously derive the quantum properties of the electrons in an atom. The wave equation gave quantum mechanics a firm mathematical footing.

Years later, physicists proved that electrons do have wave characteristics by producing the interference pattern predicted by de Broglie. Clinton Davisson, working in the United States with his junior partner Lester Germer, and George Thomson in Great Britain made the discovery. For their work, Davisson and Thomson shared a Nobel Prize in 1937. Probably no other fact brings home the dual nature of matter better than this award. George Thomson was J.J. Thomson's son. So J.J. won his Nobel for proving that electrons were particles. His son won the Prize for proving they were waves.

De Broglie's insight into the wave-particle nature of matter had a profound effect on scientists' picture of the atom. The solution to the wave equation led to a new way of looking at the atom. The old certainties of a solid electron circling a nucleus were gone. No longer could one say the electron is here or there. An electron in an atom could be anywhere, although some locations are more likely than others.

This picture—the modern picture of the atom—is hard to accept. Electrons can act as wave or particle, and their positions in an atom are governed by probabilities. The quantum mechanical view of the atom seems weird—because it is weird. But quantum mechanics beautifully explains the behavior of atoms. For example, chemists can now use quantum mechanics to predict the nature of the chemical bond that forms when atoms combine.

Although atoms are made in the stars, the millions of combinations of atoms that make up everything from plastics to mountains to tree leaves are made on Earth by chemists or geological processes or evolution. This astounding array of materials has two things in common: atoms and the chemical bonds that hold them together. Exploring the properties of those atoms and the nature of those bonds is the subject of this book.

Electrons

No chemist played a bigger role in investigating the chemical bond than Linus Pauling. Born in 1901, Pauling was studying in Europe just as Bohr, de Broglie, Einstein, Schrödinger, and others were working out quantum theory. Pauling used his knowledge of their work to pioneer the use of quantum mechanical methods in chemistry. Although he worked in many areas (including an unusual venture into medicine to explore the benefits of megadoses of vitamin C), he was best known for his work on the chemical bond.

Pauling had an outstanding career. He headed the chemistry department at Caltech for twenty years and won two Nobel Prizes. In his classic textbook, *The Nature of the Chemical Bond*, he explains how one should approach the subject. "An understanding of the electronic structure of atoms is necessary for the study of the electronic structure of molecules and the nature of the chemical bond." At its core, chemistry is about the interaction between the

**Figure 2.1
Linus Pauling, the sage
of the chemical bond**

electrons of two or more atoms to form chemical bonds. So, as Pauling says, to understand chemical bonds, one must know how the electrons in an atom behave.

BOHR'S ATOM

Early on, Niels Bohr had speculated that electrons were particles circling an atom's nucleus in quantum shells with fixed energies. Helium, he knew, has two electrons. Because it is a very stable atom, one that refuses to gain or lose electrons under most conditions, Bohr concluded that two electrons filled the lowest energy shell, which he called $n=1$. Bohr offered no reason why two electrons would completely fill that energy shell; he simply based his conclusion on the known properties of helium.

Electrons in atoms heavier than helium, Bohr hypothesized, must go into higher energy shells. Thus, lithium, with an **atomic number** of 3, would have two electrons in the $n=1$ energy shell, and the third electron must go into a new energy shell with $n=2$.

The number of electrons required to fill an atom's energy shells was first worked out by Bohr and other scientists by extending Bohr's ideas about helium to the other **noble gases**. All of these elements are extraordinarily stable. They do not react readily with other substances. This means they do not gain or lose electrons easily. Bohr and others suggested that these gases must have energy levels that are filled and unable to accept more electrons. Today, scientists know that Bohr and his colleagues were right. The lowest energy shells of every noble gas are completely filled, as shown in Table 2.1.

LINUS PAULING AND THE VITAMIN C CONTROVERSY

Linus Pauling was awarded the Nobel Prize in Chemistry in 1954 for his investigations of the chemical bond. Eight years later he won the Nobel Peace Prize for his vigorous opposition to the testing of nuclear bombs. He is the only person ever to receive two unshared Nobel Prizes.

Pauling was an impressive man, tall with perfect posture. He had a big ego, a quick mind, and an impish sense of humor. His biographer Thomas Hager tells a story that illustrates these personality traits: Jurg Waser was a chemistry professor at Caltech in 1960 who sometimes invited Pauling to act as guest lecturer. One day, knowing Pauling was coming, some students wrote on the blackboard: "Pauling is God and Waser is his Prophet." Upon spotting the graffiti, Pauling paused, then smoothly erased "and Waser is his Prophet."

Pauling was not afraid to take unpopular stands, as evidenced by his vehement protests about nuclear testing. His maverick personality led him into one of the biggest fights of his career. The subject was vitamin C, and his opponents were physicians.

In 1969, Pauling became convinced that doses of vitamin C much larger than those recommended by doctors could prevent

Bohr's electron configurations were an outgrowth of his ideas about the quantum nature of the atom. But there were problems with Bohr's theory. The biggest of these was the absence of a firm scientific foundation that left many unanswered questions: What was unique about the noble gases' filled electron shells? Why did two electrons satisfy the $n=1$ shell? Why did it take eight when

colds. The medical profession attacked his conclusions forcefully. Often, both sides cited the same studies. The studies show that vitamin C does not prevent colds, said the doctors. Yes, they do, said Pauling.

Pauling finally wearied of trying to convince medical professionals about the benefits of megadoses of vitamin C and took his case directly to the public. His book, *Vitamin C and the Common Cold*, was a best seller. Sales of the vitamin soared. Nevertheless, his dispute with physicians persisted, with Pauling advocating for huge doses of vitamin C and the medical profession pooh-poohing his ideas.

The debate still drags on, although the vitriol of the early days is gone. In June 2005, the scientific journal *PLoS Medicine* published a paper summarizing what science knows about vitamin C and the common cold. Except for one group that included people whose bodies were subject to extraordinary physical stresses—marathon runners and soldiers, for instance—most people do not benefit from huge doses of vitamin C. Although this comprehensive paper included 55 different studies, many people remain unconvinced, and Pauling no doubt would have been one of them.

TABLE 2.1 ELECTRONIC CONFIGURATIONS OF NOBLE GAS ATOMS							
ELEMENT	ATOMIC NUMBER (*Z*)	NUMBER OF ELECTRONS IN ENERGY SHELL (*n*)					
		1	2	3	4	5	6
Helium	2	2					
Neon	10	2	8				
Argon	18	2	8	8			
Krypton	36	2	8	18	8		
Xenon	54	2	8	18	18	8	
Radon	86	2	8	18	32	18	8

$n=2$? These questions were not answered until Schrödinger and his colleagues developed wave mechanics.

QUANTUM NUMBERS

Solving Schrödinger's wave equation led to a set of four **quantum numbers**. Scientists know now that these quantum numbers determine the energy and spatial distribution of electrons in an atom. The first of these is the **principal quantum number**. The principal quantum number corresponds roughly to one of Bohr's circular energy shells. It is related to the average distance of an electron from the nucleus. Following the convention Bohr started, the principal quantum number for the lowest energy shell is called $n=1$, the next $n=2$ and so on, where n is any positive whole number.

Electrons with larger values of n are more energetic and on average are farther from the nucleus. Those energetic electrons are crucial to understanding chemistry. These electrons in an atom's outermost shell are the easiest electrons to remove or share with other atoms. Thus, they are the electrons involved in chemical bonding.

The second quantum number is called the **angular momentum quantum number**. It is designated by the letter ℓ and can be thought of as representing a **subshell** within a principal energy shell. This quantum number governs the **angular momentum** (a measure of the momentum of an object moving along a curved path) of an electron and determines the shape of its **atomic orbital**, which indicates where an electron is likely to be found in the atom. The wave equation limits the angular momentum quantum number to any positive integer between 0 and $n-1$. This means that for each shell of $n=2$ or greater there are multiple subshells within the shell. For example, four subshells will be present in an energy shell with a principal quantum number of 4. Electrons in these subshells would have angular momentum quantum numbers of $\ell=0$, $\ell=1$, $\ell=2$, and $\ell=3$. Each subshell is a collection of one or more orbitals of equal energy.

Angular momentum quantum numbers are designated by the letters given in Table 2.2. The convention for identifying orbitals includes the number of the principal energy shell. In a hydrogen atom in its **ground state** (or lowest energy state), the electron would occupy a 1s orbital, where the 1 specifies the principal quantum number and the s denotes the angular momentum quantum number. If the electron jumped to the next higher energy level, its orbital would be called 2s, the most stable subshell within the $n=2$ shell. Table 2.3 shows which orbitals are allowed in the first four principal energy shells of an atom.

The third quantum number is the **magnetic quantum number**, usually designated as m_ℓ. A particle following a curved path has angular momentum. If that particle is charged (as is an electron), it creates a magnetic field. And because the angular momentum of an electron is quantized, then so is its magnetic field. Allowable values of this quantum number range from $-\ell$ to $+\ell$. A summary of the possible values for the first four quantum numbers is shown in Table 2.4.

TABLE 2.2 LETTER DESIGNATION OF SUBSHELLS (ℓ)	
VALUE OF ℓ	**LETTER**
0	s
1	p
2	d
3	f
4	g

TABLE 2.3 ALLOWABLE ORBITALS IN THE PRINCIPAL ENERGY SHELLS (n) OF AN ATOM

n	ℓ	ORBITAL LETTER	ORBITAL NAME
1	0	s	$1s$
2	0	s	$2s$
	1	p	$2p$
3	0	s	$3s$
	1	p	$3p$
	2	d	$3d$
4	0	s	$4s$
	1	p	$4p$
	2	d	$4d$
	3	f	$4f$

TABLE 2.4 QUANTUM NUMBERS FOR THE FIRST FOUR LEVELS OF ORBITALS IN THE HYDROGEN ATOM

PRINCIPAL QUANTUM NUMBER (n) (Denotes shell)	ANGULAR MOMENTUM QUANTUM NUMBER (ℓ) (Denotes subshell)	ORBITAL SHAPE DESIGNATION	MAGNETIC QUANTUM NUMBER (m_ℓ)	NUMBER OF ORBITALS
1	0	$1s$	0	1
2	0	$2s$	0	1
	1	$2p$	$-1, 0, +1$	3
3	0	$3s$	0	1
	1	$3p$	$-1, 0, +1$	3
	2	$3d$	$-2, -1, 0, +1, +2$	5
4	0	$4s$	0	1
	1	$4p$	$-1, 0, +1$	3
	2	$4d$	$-2, -1, 0, +1, +2$	5
	3	$4f$	$-3, -2, -1, 0, +1, +2, +3$	7
LIMITS OF QUANTUM NUMBERS				
$n = 1, 2, 3 \ldots$		$\ell = 0, 1, \ldots (n-1)$	$m_\ell = -\ell \ldots, 0, \ldots +\ell$	

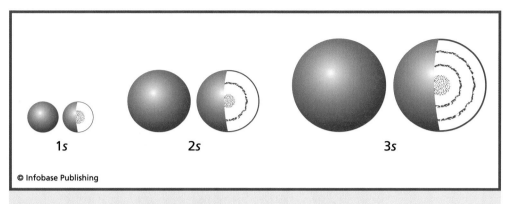

1s   2s   3s

© Infobase Publishing

Figure 2.2   The first three *s* orbitals

The magnetic quantum number determines how the *s, p, d,* and *f* orbitals are oriented in space. The shapes of the first three *s* orbitals are shown in Figure 2.2. The orbitals are spherical, with the lower-energy orbitals nested inside the higher-energy orbitals. Figure 2.3 shows the *p* and *d* orbitals. The *p* orbitals are dumbbell shaped, and all but one of the *d* orbitals have four lobes. The orbital shapes represent electron probabilities. The shaded areas are regions where an electron is most likely to be found.

The last quantum number was proposed to solve a mystery. **Emission spectroscopy** measures the wavelengths of the electromagnetic radiation emitted when an electron in an atom drops from a higher-energy state to a lower one. Spectroscopists noticed that some spectral lines split into two lines when theory predicted that only one should exist. A new quantum property and number were needed to explain spectral splitting. At the time, the electron was considered a particle, and scientists called this new property spin, usually designated as m_s. The **spin quantum number** can have only two possible values, +1/2 or −1/2. It is usually depicted as an arrow pointing either up or down.

The spin quantum number brings up a question. What physical features of the atom do the quantum numbers represent? There is no clear answer to this question because of the way quantum

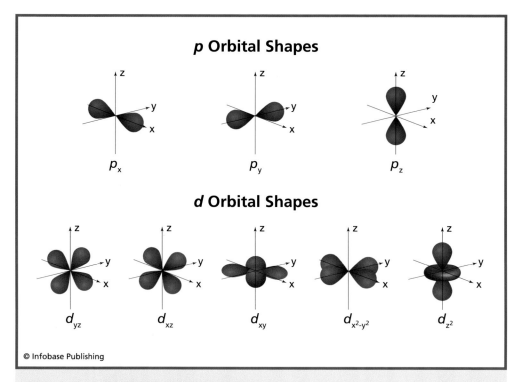

p Orbital Shapes

p_x p_y p_z

d Orbital Shapes

d_{yz} d_{xz} d_{xy} $d_{x^2-y^2}$ d_{z^2}

© Infobase Publishing

Figure 2.3   2p and 3d orbital shapes

numbers originated. Quantum numbers were first developed for the Bohr atom when electrons were considered to be negatively charged particles orbiting a nucleus. The principal energy quantum number corresponded to the average energy of the electrons in a shell of the Bohr atom. The angular momentum quantum number was associated, not surprisingly, with the angular momentum of an electron in an elliptical orbit. The magnetic quantum number was related to the behavior of electrons in a magnetic field. And spin could be visualized as an electron spinning on its own axis.

After the wave theory replaced Bohr's early ideas about the atom as a more accurate description of the subatomic world, the meanings of quantum numbers became less certain. Can a wave really spin on its own axis? No, of course not. Although it is

sometimes useful to think of quantum numbers as conferring concrete, physical characteristics to an electron, quantum properties
are only fuzzily related to things in the normal, human-sized world.
Thus, electron spin has no ordinary physical meaning. Electrons do
not spin like tops—or anything else.

BUILDING ATOMS

The principal quantum number establishes the average energy of
the electrons in an energy shell. But the energies of electrons in the
different subshells of a principal energy shell are not the same. For
the $n=3$ energy shell, the energy of each electron in the $3s$, $3p$, and $3d$
subshells is slightly different. To understand atoms and the chemical
bonds they form, it is necessary to know why.

A helium atom has two **protons** and two electrons, twice as
many of each as hydrogen. Since positive charges attract negative
charges, the nucleus of helium should exert twice as much force
on its electrons as hydrogen does. This means it should be twice as
hard to remove an electron from a helium atom as it is to remove
one from a hydrogen atom. But it is not. Instead of twice as much
energy, it takes only about 1.9 times as much.

Pulling an electron out of a helium atom takes less energy
than expected because of electron-electron repulsion. The helium
nucleus actually does pull twice as hard on its electrons as a hydrogen nucleus does, but the two electrons in helium are also repelling
one another. The net effect is to make an electron in a multi-
electron atom easier to remove than one would expect.

Because of electron repulsion, the order of the energy levels of
the atomic orbitals has a few surprises. Figure 2.4 is a diagram of
those energy levels. In some cases, the energy of an electron in an
outer orbital in a lower principal energy level is greater than that
of an electron in an inner orbital in a higher principal energy level.
An electron in a $4d$ orbital, for instance, has higher energy than
one in a $5s$ orbital. This is unexpected. It happens because electrons
in the $4d$ orbital penetrate closer to the nucleus and are repelled

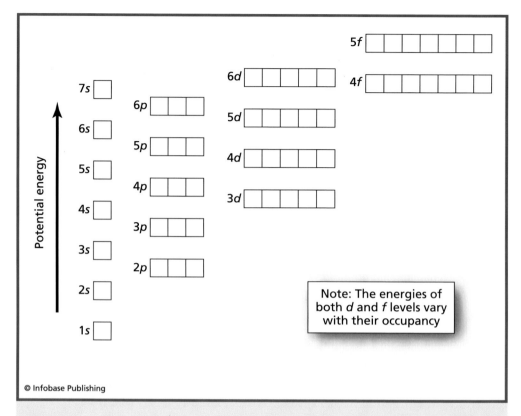

Figure 2.4   Filling in the chart determines the energy levels of atomic orbitals.

by the electrons in the inner *s* orbitals. Consequently, it takes less energy to remove an electron from a 4*d* orbital than it would take to remove one from the 5*s* orbital.

Knowing the energy levels of the orbitals makes it possible to begin figuring out the electron configurations of the elements, starting with the lightest atoms and going to heavier ones. The lightest atom is hydrogen, with one proton and one electron. So, into which orbital should that electron go? The answer, of course, is the first electron should go into a 1*s* orbital. But why? Why not a 2*s* or 3*p*? The answer comes from a rule proposed by Niels Bohr back in the 1920s. It is called the **Aufbau principle**. This principle is the first of three rules needed to predict the electron configurations of the elements. It states simply that lower-energy orbitals fill first. Looking at Figure 2.2, it is clear that the $1s$ orbital has the lowest energy. Therefore, the first electron must go there. Helium, the next lightest element, has two electrons. According to the Aufbau principle, those, too, would go in the $1s$ orbital.

The next element is lithium with three electrons. But the third electron does not go in the $1s$ orbital. The reason it does not is due to the second of the three rules, one of the most important rules in quantum mechanics. It was formulated by Wolfgang Pauli, who won a Nobel Prize in 1945. The belated prize was awarded twenty years after he proposed the rule, enabling him to finally join his colleagues—Bohr, de Broglie, Einstein, and Schrödinger—as a Nobel laureate. The rule Pauli came up with is called the **Pauli exclusion principle**, and it is what makes quantum numbers so crucial to our understanding of atoms.

The Pauli exclusion principle states that no two electrons in an atom can have the same set of quantum numbers. Each electron exists in a different quantum state. Consequently, none of the electrons in an atom can have the same energy. The $1s$ orbital has the following set of allowable numbers: $n=1$, $\ell=0$, $m_\ell=0$, $m_s=+1/2$ or $-1/2$. All of these numbers can have only one value except for spin, which has two possible states. Thus, the exclusion principle restricts the $1s$ orbital to two electrons with opposite spins. A third electron in the 1s orbital would have to have a set of quantum numbers identical to that of one of the electrons already in the orbital. So, the third electron needed for lithium must go into the next higher energy shell, which is a $2s$ orbital. The question about the Bohr atom that had so vexed scientists—why two electrons completely fill the lowest energy shell in helium—was now answered. There are only two electrons in the lowest energy shell because the quantum numbers derived from Schrödinger's equation and Pauli's principle mandate it.

The final complication in determining the electron configurations of atoms comes when we reach carbon. Carbon has six electrons. To build this atom, the first two electrons go in the $1s$ orbital, the second pair in the $2s$ orbital. The fifth electron must go into a $2p$ orbital. But into which of the three $2p$ orbitals should the sixth electron go? Into the p orbital already occupied by the fifth electron or into one of the unoccupied orbitals?

The solution to this problem and the last rule needed to generate the electron configurations for all the atoms came from a German scientist named Friedrich Hund (1896–1997). **Hund's rule** states that an atom with a higher total spin state is more stable than one with a lower spin state. Because electrons with opposite spin states cancel each other, electrons in p orbitals (and other orbitals except for s) will remained unpaired if possible. Thus, two electrons (or three, for that matter) in a p subshell would remained unpaired. So, the sixth electron in carbon-12 must have the same spin as the fifth one. The Pauli exclusion principle then requires that it fill an empty p orbital.

Knowing these three rules—the Aufbau principle, the Pauli exclusion principle, and Hund's rule—and the energy levels of the orbitals shown in Figure 2.4, it is possible to predict the electron configurations of most atoms. And these configurations are one of the keys needed to unlock the secrets of the chemical bond.

Chemists write out electron configurations by first identifying the principal quantum number, then the orbital, and finally a superscript denoting the number of electrons in that orbital. Thus, the electron configuration of a hydrogen atom would be designated as $1s^1$. Carbon-12 would be $1s^2\,2s^2\,2p^2$.

Electron configurations get more complicated in atoms with higher atomic numbers. Which orbitals the outermost electrons fill first is sometimes less than straightforward. In some cases, for instance, spin considerations can override the normal orbital filling sequence. Fortunately, though, the electron configurations of most atoms follow the normal sequence. Knowing these electron con-figurations helps chemists understand why the elements behave as they do. But long before Bohr and his colleagues came up with the modern concept of the atom, chemists had developed another way to predict the properties of the elements. It was called the periodic table of the elements, and it became and remains an indispensable tool for chemists.

THE PERIODIC TABLE

With little to guide them but hard-won laboratory experience, chemists had identified 60 or more elements by 1869. But they had no useful way of organizing them, no system for determining the elements' relationships to one another. Was there any order to the elements? The question stumped the world's best chemists until the Russian scientist Dmitri Mendeleyev solved the problem. His eureka moment did not come in his lab but in his bed. "I saw in a dream," he wrote, "a table where all the elements fell into place as required." The arrangement became the first periodic table, and its descendants adorn virtually every chemistry classroom and textbook on the planet.

Using the periodic table, Mendeleyev was able to predict the existence and properties of elements that had not yet been dis-covered. He theorized, for example, that an undiscovered element should fall in the column between silicon and tin. In 1880, a German chemist isolated a new element, which he named germanium, that had nearly the exact properties that Mendeleyev had predicted.

Central to Mendeleyev's concept of the periodic table was his conviction that the properties of the elements are a periodic func-tion of their **atomic masses**. Most periodic tables today, however, are ordered by atomic number. Although atomic numbers correlate closely with atomic mass, atomic numbers show the periodicity of the elements better because they are equal to the number of electrons in the atoms and the number of electrons governs the

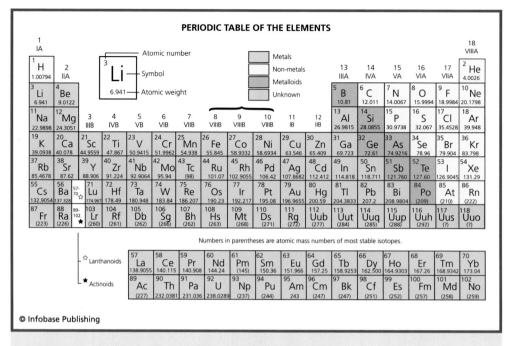

Figure 2.5 The periodic table of the elements

elements' chemical nature. The periodic table does not lead to a rigorous mathematical expression like the wave equation. The information that can be extracted from a periodic table is less precise than the solution to the wave equation. This is because its groupings contain elements with similar, but not identical, physical and chemical properties. The layout makes the relationships between the elements in each of the groups and rows obvious. It also gives the basic information about the elements that working chemists and students need: symbol, atomic number, and atomic mass.

IONIZATION ENERGY

One important relationship made clear by the periodic table is the one between atomic number and **ionization energy**. Remove one or more electrons from an atom and you get an **ion**. The energy required to remove electrons from an atom in the gaseous state is called its ionization energy. First ionization energy is the energy required to remove the highest-energy electron from an atom, the electron bound least tightly to the nucleus. Second ionization energy is the energy needed to remove the most energetic electron remaining in the atom after the first one is gone—and so on.

First ionization energies generally increase from left to right along a row in the periodic table because the increasing nuclear charge tends to hold the electrons more tightly. First ionization energies tend to decrease from the top to the bottom of a group because the increased nuclear charge is offset by higher principal energy levels and increased electron repulsion.

Ionization energies are important indicators of how atoms will behave in **chemical reactions**. Atoms with low first ionization energies, such as potassium, easily give up an electron. This means they form positive ions readily. Carbon, on the other hand, has a first ionization energy three times as large as that of potassium. So it does not give up electrons as willingly. This difference in first ionization energies has a dramatic impact on the chemical properties of **compounds** made from these two elements.

Potassium reacts vigorously with chlorine to form potassium chloride—a white, water-soluble crystalline material that is used in fertilizer manufacturing and as a sodium-free substitute for its cousin sodium chloride or table salt. But when carbon combines with chlorine to form carbon tetrachloride, the reaction product is a colorless liquid once used in fire extinguishers. It does not dissolve in water and is toxic. So do not sprinkle this sodium-free chloride on your food. Although both of these compounds are chlorides, carbon tetrachloride is as different from potassium chloride as day is from night. One reason is the big difference in the ionization energies of potassium and carbon. This difference determines the type of bond that forms between the atoms and strongly affects the properties of the resulting compounds.

Those elements with the lowest ionization energies are in Group 1 of the periodic table. These are the **alkali metals**, all of which readily give up an electron. The elements with the highest ionization energies are in Group 18. These are the noble gases, which have filled energy shells and strongly resist losing or gaining electrons. After the noble gases, the elements that cling most tightly to their electrons are their next-door neighbors in Group 17. They are called the **halogens**. Two of the elements most eager to react and exchange an electron are cesium, which is near the bottom left of the periodic table, and fluorine, at the top of the halogen group. Cesium wants to give up an electron and fluorine wants one badly. So, when cesium and fluorine are brought together, the result is what chemists like to call a vigorous reaction. Others might call it an explosion.

The first two chapters of this book have examined the characteristics of stand-alone atoms. This is a good start, but before we can understand the different types of chemical bonds, we must learn something about how atoms combine and how they behave in molecules. The next chapter explores both of those subjects.

Getting Together

Chemistry is the study of the elements and the compounds formed when they combine with one another. The two previous chapters covered the properties of atoms in isolation. This chapter will explore what happens to atoms when they interact with other atoms. It will also introduce the more practical aspects of chemistry. Although quantum mechanics is crucial to understanding chemical reactions and bonds, people were enjoying the fruits of chemistry long before Schrödinger produced his wave theory. Consider the following equation:

$$C_6H_{12}O_6 \xrightarrow{\text{enzymes}} 2\ C_2H_5OH + 2\ CO_2$$

This equation is a shorthand way of representing the reaction for the **fermentation** of a sugar (glucose) found in grapes and other substances to form carbon dioxide and ethyl alcohol, the intoxicating ingredient in wine and beer. Aside from the oxidation of wood to make fire, probably no other chemical reaction has been deliberately induced by humans for as long as this one.

No one knows the name of the imaginative person who stumbled upon the idea of fermenting grapes to make wine, but people have been using his discovery for at least 7,000 years and probably longer. Yet the complex chemistry summed up in this equation was not completely understood until the twentieth century. The 1907 Nobel Prize in Chemistry was awarded to the German Eduard Buchner for showing that the **catalyst** needed for fermentation was an **enzyme** in yeast—not the living yeast cell itself as had previously been thought.

Between those early, primitive wine makers and today's high-tech fermentation experts is a lot of chemical knowledge. This knowledge has given us more than just better-tasting wines. Our improved understanding of how matter combines spawned the modern chemical industry, which produces the materials that go into almost everything we use in our daily lives—from toothpastes and soaps to skyscrapers and jet planes.

The person who took the early steps that made this transformation from a chance fermentation to modern chemistry possible was a man named John Dalton, the descendant of English farmers and weavers.

DALTON'S ATOMIC THEORY

John Dalton was a staunch Quaker. Because Quakers were barred from attending universities, they set up their own schools, which Dalton attended. These so-called Dissenting Academies were good schools, considered better than most of the other educational institutions in England at the time. In any case, for anyone born in 1766 as Dalton was, any kind of education conferred a huge advantage. Fewer than 1 in 200 English citizens could read.

**Figure 3.1
John Dalton, early
champion of the
atomic theory**

From the beginning, Dalton showed academic promise. By age 12, he was teaching school, an occupation he would pursue for the rest of his life. Between classes he worked and thought and measured. But exactly how he developed his most important theory—the theory of atoms—is not known. In her biography, *John Dalton and the Atomic Theory*, Elizabeth Patterson recounts the muddled history of Dalton's biggest idea. "The exact path by which Dalton came to his atomic theory has been in lively debate for over a century. His own recollections are confusing and the reported accounts given later by his friends differ in important details. . . ."

What is known for sure is that by 1803, Dalton was well on the way to developing his atomic concept. He was quoted in a newspaper article in which he pinned down the date: "Nitrous oxide is composed of two particles of azote [nitrogen] and one of oxygen. This was one of my earliest atoms. I determined it in 1803, after long and patient consideration and reasoning. Chemistry began then to assume a new appearance."

Indeed, chemistry did assume a new appearance after Dalton laid down his laws. They are nothing less than the deceptively simple roots of modern chemistry.

1. Elements are composed of indivisible particles called atoms.
2. All atoms of the same element are alike and have the same mass and properties. Atoms of different elements have different masses and properties. (Dalton missed the boat a bit here. He did not know about the existence of **isotopes**, which are forms of the same element with slightly different masses due to having a different number of **neutrons** in their nuclei.)
3. Compounds form when two or more atoms combine. The elements in a compound are joined in whole-number ratios: One atom of A plus one atom of B gives a compound AB. One of A plus two of C gives AC_2, and so on.

Dalton's scientific contributions were not limited to atomic theory. He also developed the concept of **partial vapor pressure** and did important work in the area of heat theory. Upon his death in 1844 in his longtime home of Manchester, England, 40,000 people attended the funeral of this unassuming teacher and researcher.

Dalton's laws were revolutionary. First of all, they stated explicitly that atoms exist. They declared that atoms of the same elements have identical properties. Finally, they concluded with the correct definition of a compound. Although the natures of John Dalton's pragmatic atomic theory and Erwin Schrödinger's mathematically elegant wave equation were profoundly different, they stand together as two of the greatest leaps forward in the history of chemistry.

VALENCE

Dalton's laws told scientists a lot about the chemical world. But another key concept was needed to make those laws more useful. Atoms, Dalton proclaimed, combined in fixed proportions: 1:1, 1:2, 1:3, 2:3, and so on. The big question facing the chemists of the nineteenth century was figuring out what determined the proportions of each element in a compound.

Part of the answer came from an idea that had been around for a long time—the idea of **valence**. Historically, valence was associated with the eagerness with which elements combined with one another, that is, their combining power. Using crude (and inaccurate) estimates of the atomic weights of hydrogen and oxygen, Dalton concluded that a water molecule was composed of one atom of oxygen and one of hydrogen, implying that both elements had a valence of 1. By the middle of the nineteenth century Dalton's error had been corrected, and the formula was known to be H_2O. Oxygen, then, was said to have a valence of two, since it combined with two hydrogen atoms.

Mendeleyev regarded valence as a fundamental property of atoms, and he used it in constructing the periodic table. The elements in Group 1 all had a valence of 1. Those in Group 2 had a valence of 2. Over time, valence came to mean the number of bonds an atom could form. Although this method of characterizing atoms was useful to early chemists, it was poorly understood until electrons were discovered. It soon became clear that an atom's valence was related to the number of electrons it gained or lost during a chemical reaction. And because it is the electrons in an atom's outermost or most energetic electron shell that are involved in chemical reactions, those electrons are known as **valence electrons**. When oxygen reacts with hydrogen to form water, the oxygen shares two electrons with the two hydrogen atoms. This accounts for oxygen's valence of 2 and hydrogen's valence of 1. It did not, however, explain why oxygen does not gain three electrons or one.

That part of the answer had to wait until the electron configurations of the elements were known. Then, valence came to mean the number of electrons an atom must lose, gain, or share to get an outermost shell that resembles as closely as possible the outermost shell of the most stable elements, the noble gases.

Because all of the noble gases have eight electrons in their outermost shell, chemists came up with the **octet rule**. This rule states that when atoms undergo chemical reactions, they tend to do so in a way that all of the atoms in the resulting compound have eight electrons in their outer energy shells, even if they have to share some of them. The octet rule is unsophisticated compared to quantum mechanical approaches to forming compounds, and there are exceptions to it. Compounds with an odd number of valence electrons, such as nitrogen dioxide (NO_2) with 17 valence electrons spread over three atoms, for instance, do not—cannot—obey the octet rule. Yet NO_2 is a stable compound. Despite such anomalies, the rule of eight remains a simple and powerful tool for chemists to use in predicting the course of chemical reactions.

Bohr's quantized atom provided deeper insights into Dalton's law of fixed proportions. It also made it clear that the periodicity of the elements stems from their electron configurations. The system of notation commonly used to designate electron configurations is based on the noble gases. The electron configurations of the noble gases are listed in Table 2.1 in the previous chapter. The lightest noble gas is helium. Thus, the electron configuration of lithium, the next heaviest element, is written as $[He]2s^1$. This means that lithium has the electron configuration of helium plus one additional electron in the $2s$ orbital. The electron configuration of molybdenum, atomic number 42, is written $[Kr]5s^1\,4d^5$. Thus, molybdenum has the electron configuration of krypton plus one electron in the $5s$ orbital and five in $4d$ orbitals. The electron configurations of all the elements are shown on pages 106 and 107.

ELECTRONEGATIVITY

Electronegativity is a periodic feature of the elements that is almost the exact opposite of ionization energy. Ionization energy is a measure of how hard it is to remove an electron from an atom, while electronegativity is a measure of the tendency of an atom to attract electrons. The two numbers are arrived at differently, however. Ionization energy is a property of a stand-alone atom in the gaseous state. Electronegativity is a property of an atom when it is joined to another atom in a chemical bond.

Like valence, the concept of electronegativity has been around for a long time. But it was not an especially useful idea until 1932, when Linus Pauling developed a method to quantify the electronegativity of the elements. Pauling's approach was to derive a dimensionless quantity based on **bond dissociation energies**. He assigned a value of 3.98 to fluorine, the most electronegative element. Most tables of electronegativity (including the one in this book) round this number off to 4.0. Pauling then calculated the electronegativity of the other elements based on this value for fluorine.

Electronegativity decreases going down a group and generally increases going from left to right in a horizontal row (or period). Atoms with higher values of electronegativity hold electrons tightly; those with lower values give them up readily. Cesium, with a value of 0.82, is the least electronegative element; fluorine, at 4.0, is the most, apart from the noble gases. And this is why those two elements—one wanting an electron badly, the other happy to lose one—react so vigorously.

The difference in the electronegativity of two elements chemically joined in a compound determines the nature of the bond between them. When two elements with similar electronegativities combine, they tend to share electrons. In an oxygen-oxygen bond, for example, where the electronegativities of the atoms are identical, the two atoms would share two

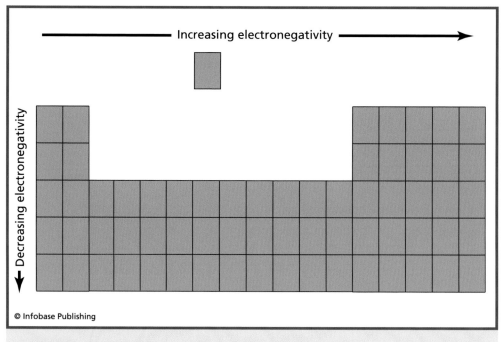

Increasing electronegativity

Decreasing electronegativity

© Infobase Publishing

Figure 3.2 Electronegativity decreases going down a group and generally increases going from left to right in a row.

valence electrons equally. Bonds of this sort are called **covalent bonds**.

Other elements, such as carbon and chlorine, with similar, but not identical, electronegativities would form covalent-like bonds. But elements with very different electronegativities would tend to have the valence electrons closer to the atom with the higher electronegativity. In the cesium fluoride example, fluorine wants to grab an electron to fill its outermost orbital, and cesium is barely holding on to one in its outermost orbital. When the two combine, the electron is not shared; it migrates from cesium to fluorine. The resulting bond is called an **ionic bond**. As was the case when potassium chloride was compared to carbon tetrachloride, the nature of the bond between two atoms—ionic in potassium chloride or covalent in carbon

CHEMICAL ANTHROPOMORPHISM

Anthropomorphism is the attribution of human-like behavior to creatures and things that are not human. In a pet store, a clerk told a customer that the turtle he was watching with his head pulled into its shell was "shy." Sure, the turtle's head was retracted, but how did the clerk know it was shy? Maybe pulling its head in was simply a turtle-like thing to do and had no significance at all. Who knows? Turtles can't talk. But you don't have to work in a pet store to anthropomorphize. Science writers do it, too.

Consider an example close at hand. The following sentence is in this chapter. ". . . fluorine wants to grab an electron to fill its outermost orbital, and cesium is barely holding on to one in its outermost orbital." Wait a minute. Does fluorine really "want" to grab an electron? Can a fluorine atom really "want" things?

Clearly, the answer is no. Atoms and molecules are not sentient beings. They don't want anything. Well, then, why do fluorine and cesium react? The answer lies in this simple statement: All systems seek to achieve a minimum of free energy.

Cesium and fluorine react because the free energy contained in a molecule of cesium fluoride is less than the free energy of the two separate atoms. When the two elements combine, most of the energy difference is given off as heat, creating the "vigorous reaction" mentioned earlier. Most scientists and science writers know this and use anthropomorphic language sparingly. The reason they use it at all is because it is a more colorful way of making a point. "Wants to grab" is more concrete and memorable than the sleeper: Cesium and fluorine react because the reaction product has lower free energy than the reactants. But both student and writer must remember that the latter is what really drives chemical reactions.

tetrachloride—plays a big role in determining the properties of the resulting compound. Both ionic and covalent bonding will be covered in depth in the following chapters.

Ionic Bonds

Let us now return to the questions that were raised in Chapter 1 concerning the properties of sodium, chlorine, and sodium chloride. Could three substances be more different? How can a very reactive, silvery metal combine with a poisonous yellowish gas to produce the white, crystalline solid called table salt? How could an element with a melting point of 98°C unite with another element with a melting point of –101°C to create a compound with a melting point of 801°C, far above the melting points of both of its constituents? Clearly, when sodium and chlorine combine, the result is something entirely different from either sodium or chlorine. Even more interestingly, sodium chloride's properties are not an average of the properties of sodium and chlorine. No, the compound made from the two elements resembles neither element nor some average between them. When sodium and chlorine combine, they form a brand-new substance.

Why should this be? Mix red and yellow paints together and you get orange, a blend of the two colors. Add 10 grams (g) of iron pellets to 10g of aluminum pellets, mix thoroughly, and divide into two equal piles. The result is as one would expect: Each pile is a mixture containing about 5g of iron and 5g of aluminum. Why do combining atoms act differently from colors or pellets of metals?

The answer lies in the nature of the atoms. Chemically combining atoms changes the atoms themselves. Stand-alone atoms and atoms in compounds have different properties. And what changes the atoms are the bonds between them. To a large extent, the electronegativities of the atoms in a compound determine the type of bond that forms. An atom with a high electronegativity, such as chlorine, holds electrons more tightly than an atom with low electronegativity, such as sodium. Thus, when sodium and chlorine combine, the electron in the $3s$ orbital of sodium moves to the chlorine and fills its $3p$ orbital. This migration leaves the two atoms in stable, low energy electron configurations. Both have eight electrons in their outer energy shells just like our old friends, the very stable noble gases.

The migration of an electron dramatically changes the nature of the atoms involved. In fact, they are no longer called atoms; they are called **ions**.

$$Na \text{ (atom)} \rightarrow Na^+ \text{ (ion)} + e^-$$

$$Cl \text{ (atom)} + e^- \rightarrow Cl^- \text{ (ion)}$$

Combining the two equations yields:

$$Na + Cl \rightarrow Na^+ + Cl^-$$

In an electrolytic system in which a current passes between two poles, the positively charged sodium ions migrate to the **cathode**, the negatively charged pole. Because of this ions with a positive charge are called **cations**. Negatively charged ions migrate to the positively charged pole, or **anode**, and are called **anions**.

COULOMB'S LAW

The formation of ions explains how a poisonous gas can combine with a highly reactive metal to form the white, crystalline substance called table salt. The French physicist Charles-Augustin de Coulomb (1736–1806) played a big role in helping chemists to understand why ions behave so differently from atoms. It started with one of Coulomb's inventions, a vastly improved, extremely sensitive **torsion balance** (see Figure 4.1).

Coulomb charged the **pith balls** in the apparatus with electrostatic charges. The first charged ball was fixed in place; the second was attached to a horizontal bar suspended by a fiber or wire. When the two balls had like charges, they repelled one another. The force of that repulsion was measured by the distance between the two balls, which was the point where the tension in the twisting fiber equaled the force of repulsion. Using this difficult, sensitive instrument, Coulomb came up with the law now named for him.

$$F = K \bullet q_1 q_2 / r^2$$

In this equation, F is the force of repulsion between two charged objects (If the objects have opposite charges, then F is the force of attraction.); q_1 and q_2 represent the magnitude of the electrical charges on the objects; r is the distance between them; and k is the electrostatic constant. The variable that plays a big role in determining the strength of ionic bonds is r, the distance between two charged objects. As r gets smaller, the force gets larger. And because the distance between ions in a chemical bond is small indeed, the force holding the oppositely charged ions Na^+ and Cl^- together is a strong one.

How close are the positive and negative ions in a crystal of salt? Scientists have measured the distance between them. They

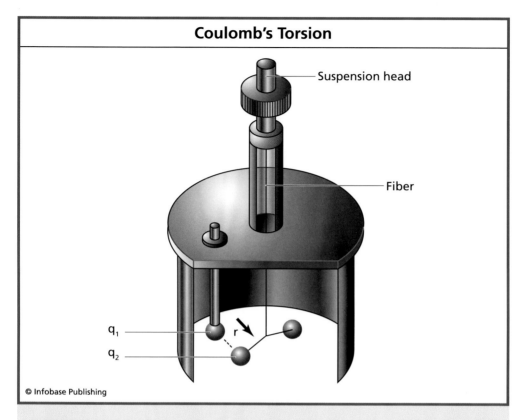

Coulomb's Torsion

Suspension head

Fiber

q_1

r

q_2

© Infobase Publishing

Figure 4.1 **In this setup, two charged pith balls repel one another. Coulomb used this apparatus to come up with a law that determines the force of repulsion between two charged objects. In this diagram q^1 and q^2 represent the magnitude of the electrical charge on each pith ball, and r represents the distance between the two pith balls.**

are 0.0000000236 meters or 0.236 nanometers apart from center to center. The reason they are not even closer together is because the attractive force between the oppositely charged ions is balanced by the repelling force of the electron clouds of the two ions. Thus, both the attractive and the repelling forces in an ionic crystal are governed by Coulomb's Law.

The equation for Coulomb's Law resembles the inverse square law developed by Isaac Newton to calculate the gravitational attraction between two bodies

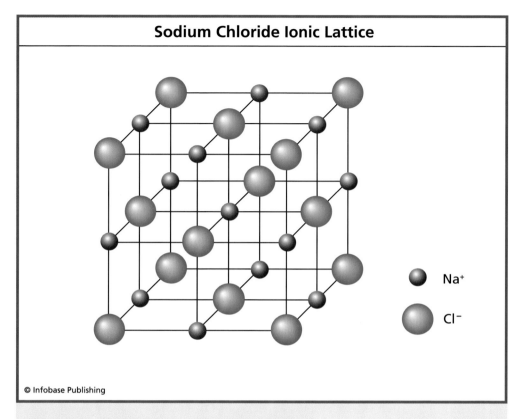

Sodium Chloride Ionic Lattice

Na⁺

Cl⁻

© Infobase Publishing

Figure 4.2   The ionic lattice of sodium chloride

$$F = \frac{GM_1M_2}{r^2}$$

However, the electrostatic attraction between two charged particles is many trillions of times stronger than the gravitational force. Recall that it was the strong electrostatic attraction between a proton and an electron in the hydrogen atom that made Bohr's original picture of the atom "impossible" and led to the quantum theory of atoms.

The strength of the ionic bond in sodium chloride arises from the electrostatic attraction between the sodium and chloride ions. These strong bonds explain why the properties of sodium chloride are so different from those of its constituent elements. For example,

PITH BALLS? WHAT IS PITH?

Pith is the spongy material in the center of the stems of most plants. Because dry pith is light in weight and readily takes an electrical charge, it has been long used in electrostatic research and for demonstrations of Coulomb's Law. (These days, however, pith has been largely replaced by those readily available lightweight balls of plastic packing materials that are ubiquitous in the modern world.) For a typical classroom demonstra-

Figure 4.3   An explorer in a pith helmet

tion, attach a thin string to each of two pith balls and suspend them on a stand. Rub a glass rod with a piece of silk cloth. The silk removes electrons from the rod, leaving it positively charged. Touch the pith balls with the rod. This transfers a positive charge to the balls, which will repel one another and spring apart.

To see a more glamorous use of pith, catch one of those old black-and-white movies that feature African explorers or big game hunters. Almost without exception, the men and women traipsing through the jungle in these movies wore odd-looking hats called pith helmets. Developed in the middle of the nineteenth century, pith helmets provided a lightweight shield against sun and rain. After a few decades, pith was replaced by the more durable cork. But despite the absence of pith in the hat, the name remains. And though the pith helmet itself has declined in popularity, they can still be found on the heads of intrepid explorers tromping through the black-and-white jungles of yesteryear.

TABLE 4.1 PROPERTIES OF SODIUM, CHLORINE, AND TABLE SALT			
	SODIUM	**CHLORINE**	**SODIUM CHLORIDE**
Symbol	Na	Cl	NaCl
Molar mass (g/mol)	23.0	35.4	58.4
Appearance (type of element or state of matter)	silvery (metal)	yellowish-green (gas)	white crystalline (solid)
Melting point			
°C	98	−101	801
°F	208	−151	1,474
Solubility in water at 25°C (g/100 mL)	reacts violently	0.4	35.9
Electronegativity	1.0	3.0	N/A
Electron Configuration	$[Ne]3s^1$	$[Ne]3s^23p^5$	N/A

the melting point of sodium chloride, as shown in Table 4.1, is much higher than that of either sodium or chlorine. The tightly bound ions in a sodium chloride crystal means the temperature must be raised quite high before the ions gain enough **kinetic energy** to escape the rigid crystalline structure. The pure elements of sodium and chlorine, however, are composed of electrically neutral atoms. And because there is no ionic bonding, they melt at much lower temperatures.

One peculiarity of salt (and other substances with atoms locked in a crystalline structure by ionic bonds) is that individual molecules of sodium chloride do not exist at room temperature. What does exist is a lattice of oppositely charged ions, a crystal held together by the strong electrostatic attraction between ions.

BEYOND SALT

The difference in electronegativity between two atoms in a compound determines the type of bond between them. In the chlorine-chlorine bond, for example, the two atoms have no difference in electronegativity and would form a pure covalent bond with shared electrons. In the case of sodium and chlorine, however, the electronegativity difference is a quite large 2.0. This means that sodium can achieve a more stable, lower-energy state by completely giving up its outermost electron to a chlorine atom, forming an ionic bond.

There is a middle ground between the purely covalent and purely ionic bonds. These are called **polar covalent bonds**. They will be covered in the next chapter along with pure covalent bonds.

Most elements form bonds with some covalent character. But when the alkali metals of Group 1 react with the halogens in Group 17, the result is usually a strong ionic bond. This is because the alkali metals readily lose an electron, and the halogens are eager to gain one. But not all of the alkali metal **halides** form pure ionic bonds. Lithium iodide, for example, is a white crystalline salt that is soluble in water and resembles table salt. But its melting point is 350°C, much lower than that of sodium chloride. Furthermore, lithium iodide dissolves in some organic solvents, which well-behaved ionic bonded substances like sodium chloride never do. The Li-I bond can be thought of as an ionic bond with some covalent character.

Some of the halides of the **alkaline earth metals** have a similar identity problem. Calcium chloride and magnesium chloride have melting points almost as high as that of sodium chloride. Those compounds are clearly held together by ionic bonds. Beryllium chloride, on the other hand, melts at about half the temperature of table salt. And it boils at 520°C compared to salt's 1,465°C. The differences in properties are due to the partially covalent bond formed between beryllium and chlorine.

Fortunately, chemists do not have to memorize which compounds do or do not have ionic bonds. A simple rule of thumb helps them to gauge the type of bond that forms between two atoms. All one needs is an electronegativity table, such as Table 3.2 in the previous chapter. Experience has shown that when the difference in electronegativity of two atoms is equal to or greater

TABLE 4.2 BOND POLARITIES		
BOND	ELECTRONEGATIVITY DIFFERENCES	TYPE OF BOND
H-H	0	covalent
Cl-Cl	0	covalent
C-H	0.4	weakly polar covalent
O-H	1.4	polar covalent
Li-I	1.5	strongly polar covalent
Be-Cl	1.5	strongly polar covalent
Mg-Cl	1.7	ionic
Ca-Cl	2.0	ionic
Na-Cl	2.0	ionic

than 1.7, the bond will likely be ionic. (This is a very rough rule of thumb; some chemists use a difference as high as 2.0 to distinguish ionic from covalent bonds.) Differences of less than 1.7 result in bonds with some covalent characteristics. Table 4.2 shows the electronegativity difference between selected atoms and gives the nature of the bond formed between them.

With an electronegativity table, establishing the ionic or covalent nature of the bond between two atoms is just a matter of simple subtraction. However, there is more to understanding the chemical bond than just knowing the electronegativity of atoms. Several other bond variations will be covered in the next chapter.

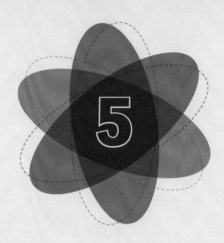

Sharing Electrons: The Covalent Bond

Ionic bonding is easy to visualize. One electron (or more) moves from atom A to atom B, leaving A with a positive charge and B with a negative charge. The resulting lattice of ions is held together by electrostatic forces whose strength is dictated by Coulomb's law. Covalent bonds are more varied and more complicated.

LEWIS DOT STRUCTURES

Covalent bonds form between atoms with similar electronegativities. In compounds held together by covalent bonds, electrons don't migrate from one atom to another as they do in ionic bonds. Instead, they are shared by the atoms in the molecule. One way to visualize this was proposed by Gilbert Lewis, a chemist at the University of California, Berkeley. His representations of molecular bonds are called **Lewis dot structures**. These

GILBERT NEWTON LEWIS (1875–1946)

Although most chemistry students know about Lewis dot structures, few of them know much about the man who invented those dotty structures. Fewer still can identify his most important contribution to valence bond theory.

Figure 5.1   Chemical structures innovator Gilbert Lewis

Lewis was an excellent student, earning his Ph.D. at Harvard by the age of 24. He taught for a while at M.I.T., then moved west to Berkeley in 1912 to become the chairman of the chemistry department at the University of California, a position he held until he died.

Lewis's research was wide-ranging and outstanding. He published important papers on chemical bonds, acid-base theory, and thermodynamics. He also developed firm ideas about how to build a chemistry department. His philosophy of education was something less than egalitarian. Writing in the *Journal of Chemical Education*, the distinguished chemist Gerald Branch spelled out Lewis's ideas: "[F]or a chemist to be useful to the world he should have a superior mind. . . . the department [should] use its time and energy on good rather than average students." Although Lewis was criticized for his tough-minded

continues

continued

approach to educating chemists, he built a strong department that produced several Nobel Prize winners.

Lewis himself never won a Nobel, although many of his colleagues thought he deserved one for his many contributions to valence bond theory. His key insight came in 1916, fewer than twenty years after J.J. Thomson discovered the electron. Linus Pauling—the guru of the chemical bond—summed up Lewis's most important contribution. It was, Pauling said, "the idea that the chemical bond consists of a pair of electrons held jointly by two atoms."

structures use dots to denote the valence electrons of an element or molecule.

Lewis conceived these representational structures in the early twentieth century when chemists still believed that electrons were tiny objects whirling around a nucleus. The wave picture of the atom has since superseded the solar system atom, but Lewis structures are still helpful in visualizing and understanding chemical reactions.

The Lewis dot structures for hydrogen, oxygen, and water are shown below.

$$2 \, H\odot + \, \ddot{\underset{..}{O}} \longrightarrow \ddot{\underset{\odot}{O}}\odot H$$
$$H$$

• Oxygen electron

⊙ Hydrogen electron

POLAR COVALENT BONDS

Not all covalent bonds share electrons equally. If two atoms have the same electronegativity, then the bond between them will be purely covalent, with the shared electrons being distributed evenly between the atoms. Hydrogen, for instance, occurs as two joined atoms, H-H. Because both atoms in the molecule have the same electronegativity, they form a covalent bond with the two electrons being shared equally.

Water, on the other hand, is composed of two different elements. Oxygen is considerably more electronegative than hydrogen, but not so different as to completely capture hydrogen's electron. Nevertheless, the higher electronegativity of oxygen pulls the shared electrons more strongly than hydrogen does. Covalent bonds such as this one have some ionic character. In the case of water, that means that the oxygen atom has a small negative charge and the hydrogen atoms are slightly positive. These less-than-full charges are represented here by the symbol δ, which means "partial." An atom labeled δ⁻, for example, has a negative charge that is less than the amount of charge that a negative ion (anion) would possess. Of course, the charges cancel each other out leaving the molecule itself electrically neutral. However, this separation of charges creates an **electric dipole** along the bond axis, and the bonds that exhibit this slight separation of charges within a molecule are called polar covalent bonds.

One important result of polar covalent bonding is that it encourages bonding between molecules. In this intermolecular bonding, the negative end of one molecule attracts the positive end of another. These bonds are very weak compared to the bonds between atoms in a molecule, but they confer crucially important properties to some substances, including water and our own **DNA**. In fact, intermolecular bonds are so important that they get their own chapter later in the book. The next section of this chapter will explore other types of covalent bonds.

COORDINATE COVALENT BONDS

There is often an unstated assumption that the shared electrons in a covalent bond come from different atoms. In the hydrogen molecule, for example, each atom donates one electron to the H-H bond. But a single covalent bond is simply two shared electrons. Nothing prevents both electrons in the bonding pair from originating with the same atom. When both of the electrons in a shared pair come from one atom, the bond is called a **coordinate covalent bond**.

Ammonia (NH_3) is a common substance that forms coordinate covalent bonds. When ammonia is dissolved in water and hydrochloric acid (HCl) is added, the following reaction takes place.

$$H:\overset{..}{\underset{..}{Cl}}: + H:\overset{..}{\underset{H}{N}}:H \longrightarrow \left[H:\overset{H}{\underset{H}{\overset{..}{N}}}:H \right]^{+} + \left[:\overset{..}{\underset{..}{Cl}}: \right]^{-}$$

The resulting compound, NH_4Cl, is an ionic-bonded **salt**. The salt's ammonium cation (NH_4^+) is held together by covalent bonds, one of which formed when a hydrogen ion united with the pair of unshared electrons on the nitrogen atom. Keep in mind that three of the nitrogen-hydrogen bonds in ammonia formed as ordinary covalent bonds, in which each element contributed one electron, while the fourth formed as a coordinate covalent bond with both electrons coming from the nitrogen. Nevertheless, in the assembled ammonium ion (NH_4^+), the four nitrogen-hydrogen bonds are identical. No matter the source of the paired electrons, the bonds that form are the same.

Coordinate bonds are just one of several covalent bond types, as the next section will illustrate.

DOUBLE BONDS, TRIPLE BONDS, AND RESONANCE

The more complex molecules examined here require a new way to specify their structure. A simple example is water, represented by the **molecular formula**, H_2O. This tells a chemist that this molecule is made of two atoms of hydrogen and one of oxygen. But it does not tell how the atoms are arranged. Throughout this book, the structure of water has been assumed to be HOH, with the two hydrogen atoms attached to the oxygen. But based solely on the molecular formula, H_2O could have a different structure— HHO—with a bond between the two hydrogen atoms and another between one of the hydrogen atoms and the oxygen. A Lewis dot structure would show how this molecule is put together, but with big, complicated molecules, drawing Lewis dot structures is cumbersome.

Modern **structural formulas** use a dash to indicate a covalent bond made up of a shared pair of electrons. The structural formula for water is H—O—H. The structural formulas for a few other common substances are shown below.

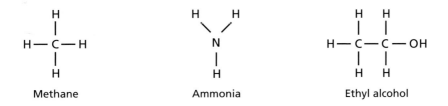

Methane   Ammonia   Ethyl alcohol

To fill their energy shells and reach a lower energy state, atoms sometimes share more than one pair of electrons. Oxygen, for example, has six electrons in its outer valence shell. The most common form of atmospheric oxygen is O_2. For both atoms to complete their electron shells, they must share two pairs of electrons. The reaction to form the molecule and its structure would then be represented as:

$$:\ddot{O}: + :\ddot{O}: \longrightarrow :\ddot{O}::\ddot{O}: \quad \text{or} \quad O + O \longrightarrow O = O$$

In the structural formula for O_2, the sharing of two pairs of electrons, called a **double bond**, is represented by two parallel dashes. Sometimes three pairs of electrons are shared, producing a **triple bond**, which is indicated by three parallel dashes.

N_2	C_2H_2	HCN
$N \equiv N$	$H - C \equiv C - H$	$H - C \equiv N$
Nitrogen	Acetylene	Hydrogen cyanide

Resonance Structures

Sometimes there is more than one correct structural formula for a compound with double or triple bonds. Ozone, for example, can be correctly written as one of two forms.

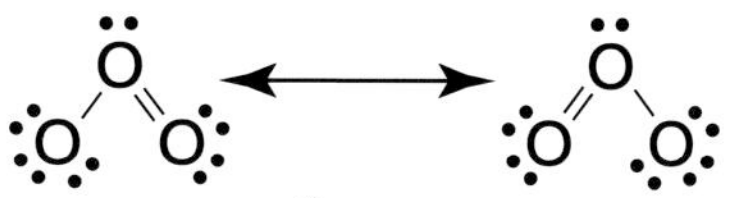

Ozone

Another example is benzene, a cyclic **aromatic compound**.

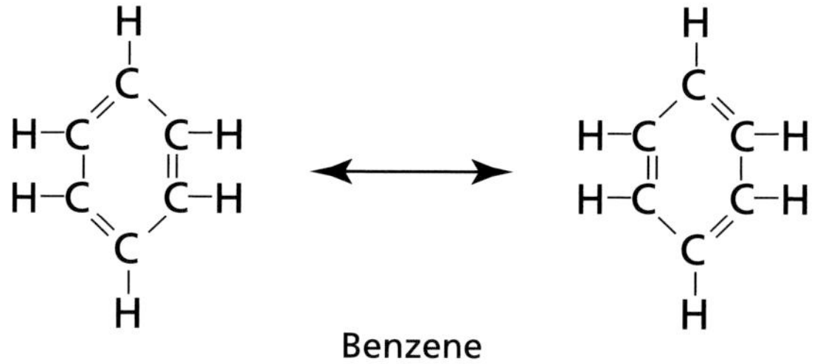

Benzene

Which of these two structures for benzene is correct? The answer is neither. Benzene has a **resonance structure** that lies somewhere between the two forms and is different from both of them. The word "resonance" is a bit misleading because it implies that benzene is oscillating back and forth between two forms. But when the distance between the atoms in benzene is measured, the carbon-carbon bond lengths are all the same. Resonance structures have only one form, a resonance hybrid somewhere between the two possibilities.

Resonance structures result from a phenomenon known as **electron delocalization**. The electron pairs represented by the three double bonds in a benzene ring are delocalized. These electrons belong to no particular atom or bond. As a consequence, no ordinary double bonds exist in a benzene ring. The six electrons that make up the second parts of each double bond are in a set of 3 orbitals that extend across the entire molecule. This smear of electrons is usually represented as a circle within the ring.

Resonance structures of molecules are more stable than the hypothetical static forms from which they are derived. When orbitals extend over an entire molecule, the electrons in the expanded orbitals can have longer wavelengths and correspondingly lower energy. The ideas behind delocalization led scientists to a more rigorous approach to understanding the covalent bond than the methods covered so far. That approach is called **molecular orbital** theory.

MOLECULAR ORBITALS

The structural formulas used to represent molecules are based on valence bond theory. Double and triple bonds simply represent additional pairs of shared valence electrons. But structural formulas, while useful, don't tell the whole story about the nature of the bonds between atoms in a molecule. Valence bond theory falls flat when it tries to explain delocalized electrons and resonance structures. To get at what is really going on inside molecules, chemists had to dig deeper.

The Lewis dot structure and the molecular formula for the simplest molecule, H_2, are

$$H - H \qquad H : H$$

But what do these structures mean in terms of how the electrons are distributed in the hydrogen molecule? Electrons are not dashes or dots. Nor are they tiny charged particles circling an atomic nucleus. What actually happens when the clouds of valence electrons of atoms merge to form a molecule? The answer is that the molecule develops its own orbitals, called molecular orbitals, which can be described as a combination of the valence orbitals of the atoms in the molecule.

To calculate the molecular orbitals of the hydrogen molecule, the orbital equations of the two atoms are combined. When the orbital equations are added together, the result is a bonding molecular orbital that extends over both atoms. Subtracting the orbital equations of the atoms produces an antibonding molecular orbital. This process is called the **linear combination of atomic orbitals** or LCAO. It gives a more sophisticated and accurate approximation of how electrons behave in a molecule than the valence bond approach. It is also more difficult to use, so chemists choose the method that is adequate for their particular purpose.

Our study of LCAO theory begins with the simplest molecule. When two hydrogen atoms come together, their two spherical s orbitals interact to form a dumbbell-shaped molecular orbital. When that orbital is occupied by two electrons, it is called a sigma bond. The sigma bond gets it name because it appears spherical, like an s orbital, when viewed along the bonding axis. (Sigma is the English word for the Greek letter σ, which corresponds to the English letter s.)

The bonding orbital in a hydrogen molecule produces a high electron density between the two positively charged nuclei. This high electron density mediates the repulsion between the nuclei and gives the molecule a lower energy than that of the reacting atoms. Thus, energy must be added to break the hydrogen atoms apart. The antibonding orbital, however, provides for a low electron density between the nuclei. If electrons were in the antibonding orbital, they would destabilize the molecule. However, both elec-

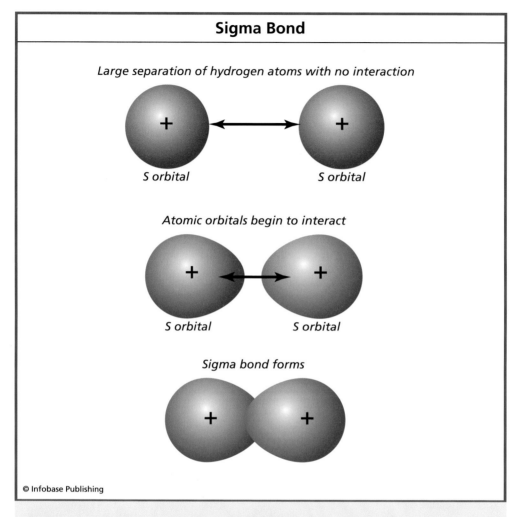

Sigma Bond

Large separation of hydrogen atoms with no interaction

S orbital   S orbital

Atomic orbitals begin to interact

S orbital   S orbital

Sigma bond forms

© Infobase Publishing

Figure 5.2   The formation of a sigma bond between two hydrogen atoms.

trons of the H_2 molecule occupy the bonding orbital. The shapes and energies of the two orbital types are illustrated in Figure 5.2.

In addition to explaining why hydrogen bonds with itself, LCAO theory also explains why some atoms do not. A beryllium atom, for instance, has four electrons, including two valence electrons in the 2s orbital. It would seem that the 2s orbitals of two beryllium atoms could join together to form a sigma bond.

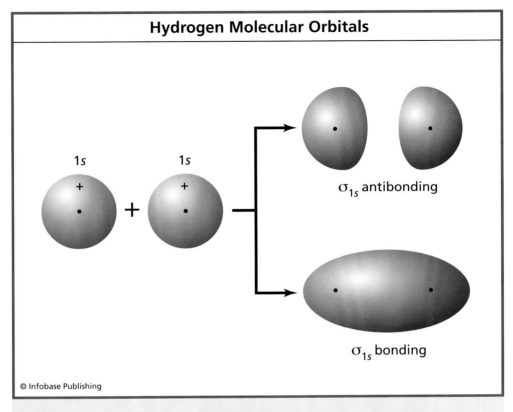

Figure 5.3   Bonding and antibonding molecular orbitals of hydrogen

However, the Pauli exclusion principle allows only two electrons in each orbital. To form Be_2, two electrons would have to fill the bonding orbital. The other two would have to fill the antibonding orbital. When the energies of the two orbitals are added together, the total energy of Be_2 molecule would equal that of the isolated atoms. Because a combination of the two atoms would not reduce the free energy of the system, the reaction would not proceed.

Atoms with p orbitals can also form sigma bonds. Fluorine ($1s^2\, 2s^2\, 2p^5$) has one p orbital that is half-filled. When one fluorine atom reacts with another fluorine, their two p orbitals can overlap end-to-end to form a bond that is symmetrical along the bonding axis.

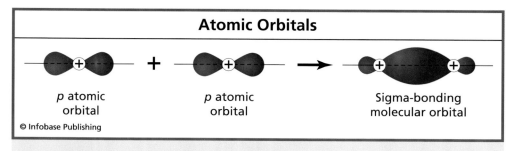

Atomic Orbitals

p atomic orbital   *p* atomic orbital   Sigma-bonding molecular orbital

© Infobase Publishing

Figure 5.4   *P* orbitals that form a sigma bond

The remaining two *p* orbitals in each fluorine are oriented perpendicularly to the first *p* orbital. When two perpendicular *p* orbitals—one on each fluorine—overlap in a side-by-side configuration, they form a pi bond as shown in Figure 5.6. This bond is named after the Greek letter π, which it resembles, at least a little. The electron clouds in pi bonds overlap less than those in sigma bonds, and they are correspondingly weaker.

Molecular orbital theory explains much about molecules. It can tell a chemist how far apart the atoms are, the angles of the bonds between them, and the energy of the bond. But applying molecular orbital theory requires the manipulation of its constituent atoms' complicated wave functions, a cumbersome process requiring sophisticated numerical computations. That's why two easier, but less rigorous, methods for getting at the arrangements of atoms in a molecule have been developed.

The **hybridized orbital** approach is a simplified way of predicting the geometry of a molecule with three or more atoms by mixing the valence orbitals of its central atom. An alternative approach, **valence shell electron-pair repulsion (VSEPR)** theory, accomplishes the same thing in a more qualitative way.

Let us start by using the hybrid orbital method to predict the structure of methane. Methane, CH_4, is composed of a carbon atom and four hydrogen atoms. The carbon atom has an electron configuration of $1s^2\ 2s^2\ 2p^2$. Each hydrogen atom has an electron configuration of $1s^1$. Experiments showed that the geometry of the

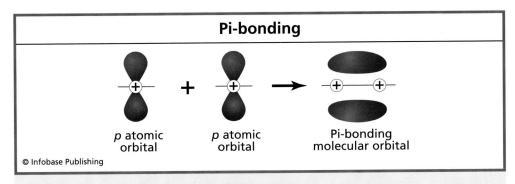

Pi-bonding

p atomic orbital

p atomic orbital

Pi-bonding molecular orbital

© Infobase Publishing

Figure 5.5 *p* **orbitals that form a pi bond**

methane molecule is tetrahedral, with all of the carbon-hydrogen bond distances being equal. Chemists needed a simpler way than the complete molecular orbital treatment to answer this question: How can hydrogen combine with carbon's *s* and *p* orbitals, which are quite different in shape and length, to produce a molecule with with four equal bond lengths?

To explain this result, Linus Pauling, who had his hand in most of the important work on the chemical bond, suggested in 1931 that the atomic orbitals of carbon (and other atoms) hybridize during a chemical reaction. Instead of its *s* orbitals and *p* orbitals interacting with hydrogen, carbon forms four identical hybrid orbitals called sp^3 orbitals. These orbitals each have a large lobe that points toward a vertice of a tetrahedron Each of these orbitals combines with an *s* orbital of a hydrogen atom to form four equal sigma bonds. The result is the tetrahedral structure shown in Figure 5.6 with all bond lengths the same. The bond lengths and bond angles predicted by the hybridized structure fit the experimental data nicely. Since then, the concept of hybridization has been extended to other atomic orbitals.

The other approach to molecular geometry is VSEPR theory. This theory holds that the shapes of molecules are determined by the repulsion between electron pairs around a central atom. Consider the bonding angle between two hydrogen atoms in a water molecule. One would a expect a 90° angle if hydrogen formed two

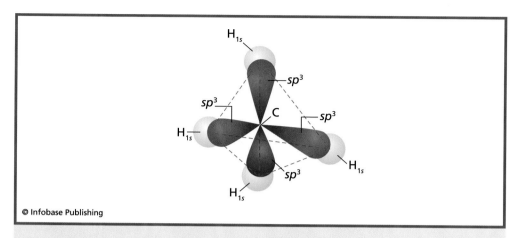

© Infobase Publishing

Figure 5.6   The tetrahedral structure of methane

sigma bonds with the *p* orbitals of oxygen, which are at right angles to one another. The actual angle of 105° is explained by the repulsion between the valence electron pairs. The repulsion produces a tetrahedral structure for water, with two positions around the oxygen atom occupied by hydrogen atoms and the other two by unbonded electron pairs. This molecular structure is described as "bent."

VSEPR theory works best when predicting the shapes of molecules composed of a central atom surrounded by bonded atoms and unbonded electrons.

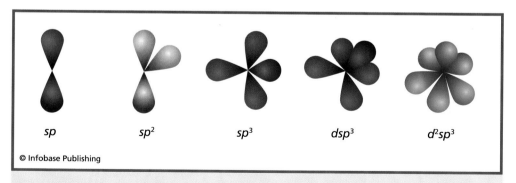

© Infobase Publishing

Figure 5.7   The orbital shapes of different types of hybridized orbitals

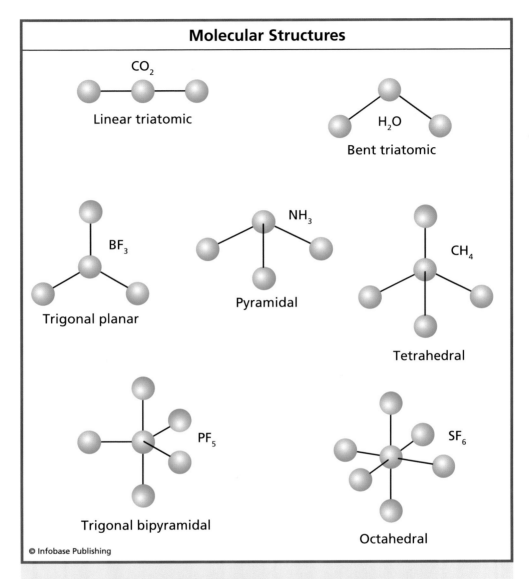

Molecular Structures

CO_2

Linear triatomic

H_2O

Bent triatomic

BF_3

Trigonal planar

NH_3

Pyramidal

CH_4

Tetrahedral

PF_5

Trigonal bipyramidal

SF_6

Octahedral

© Infobase Publishing

Figure 5.8   Different molecular shapes for molecules with a central atom.

Covalent and ionic are the most basic bond types. Together they offer a smörgåsbord of ways to hold molecules together. But to explain the behavior of metals, yet a third type of bond is needed. It will be covered in the next chapter.

The Metallic Bond

What is a metal? The answer to this seemingly simple question turns out to be a bit slippery. As usual, the periodic table is a good place to begin looking for answers. The periodic table, shown on pages 102 and 103, is divided into three types of elements: the metals, the **nonmetals**, and the **metalloids**. The table, however, tells us nothing about why tin is a metal but its next-door neighbor antimony is a metalloid. Or why silicon is called a metalloid but neighboring phosphorus is classified as a nonmetal.

One feature of metals is well known. Metals tend to lose electrons to nonmetals in a chemical reaction. That is, they tend to have lower electronegativities than nonmetals. This is obvious in compounds formed from metals at the far left of the periodic table and nonmetals from the far right. Sodium (a metal) clearly loses an electron to chlorine (a nonmetal) forming an ionic bond. The resulting compound—table salt—is a water-soluble, white crystalline substance, which are characteristics of ionic-bonded compounds.

But the nature of the compounds formed when the metal and nonmetal are closer to the center of the periodic table is less obvious. Their electronegativities are closer together. And the electronegativity difference between the atoms in a compound determines the nature of the bond. Recall that differences of 1.7 or more result in ionic bonds; atoms with differences less than 1.7 form bonds with some covalent character. Lead sulfide (PbS) is an example of such a compound. Lead has an electronegativity of 1.9; sulfur is 2.5. The difference of 0.6 is less than 1.7, so the bond between them should have some covalent character. Like sodium chloride, lead sulfide is a crystalline compound. However, it is dark and shiny, quite unlike salt. It is also insoluble in water, which indicates a high degree of covalency in the lead-sulfur bond, just as one would expect.

PROPERTIES OF METALS

So, if both sodium and lead are defined as metals and chlorine and sulfur as nonmetals, why is sodium chloride so different from lead sulfide? Something appears to be missing in our definition of a metal. It is true that metals tend to lose electrons to nonmetals in a chemical reaction, but that definition turns out to be so broad that it is not very useful. How, then, should a metal be defined? The answer was arrived at years before the electronic structure of atoms was known. Simply put, metals are best defined by their common physical properties:

1. *High electrical conductivity.* The conductivity of metals is many **orders of magnitude** higher than that of nonmetals. Sulfur, for example, is considered an **electrical insulator**, while aluminum, only three places to its left in the periodic table, is a good conductor of electricity.
2. *High density.* Metals are usually much denser than nonmetals. Sodium, for instance, has a density of 0.97

grams per cubic centimeter at room temperature, while chlorine—with a higher molecular mass—is a gas with a density of .0032 g cc^{-1}. The metal tin is almost 50% denser than iodine, its nonmetal neighbor in the periodic table.

3. *Highly lustrous.* Metals are shiny; nonmetals are not—at least most of them are not. A notable exception is the form of carbon known as diamond.

4. *Electron emission.* Many metals emit electrons when exposed to electromagnetic radiation. This is the famous photoelectric effect discussed in Chapter 1. Einstein's study of this effect led him to conclude that light could act as either wave or particle.

5. *Highly ductile and malleable.* Metals can withstand large deformations without fracturing. They can be drawn into wires, hammered into horseshoes, or bent into paper clips.

The list makes it clear that a bar of copper or iron has properties that are entirely different from substances held together by ionic or covalent bonds. This chapter aims to show that the source of these properties is the **metallic bond**. But what kind of bonding would make metals dense and conduct electricity readily? What sort of structure would make them lustrous and malleable? Why should metals eject electrons when a light is shined on them?

BONDING IN METALS

The most important clue to understanding the nature of the metallic bond is the high electrical conductivity of metals. Like most substances held together by ionic or covalent bonds, pure salt and pure water do not conduct electricity well. But pure copper does. Scientists could not make much sense of this difference until J.J. Thomson discovered the electron in 1897. Soon afterward, scientists figured out that an electric current is the flow of electrons and that electrical conductivity is a measure of how free the electrons are to move. The high conductivity of metals indicates that their electrons are not tightly bound to atoms and are therefore freer to move than the electrons in substances with ionic or covalent bonds.

The freedom of electrons to move easily coupled with the metals' high density led scientists to hypothesize that metals were tightly packed lattices (giving high density) of positively charged **ion cores** immersed in a sea of freely moving valence electrons (giving high electrical conductivity). An ion core is neither atom nor ion. It is an atomic nucleus surrounded by all but one or two of its electrons. Those electrons are tightly bound to the nucleus, and are not part of the sea of mobile electrons that surrounds them. The electron sea acts as the glue that mediates the repulsion of the ion cores and holds the lattice together. The positively charged ion cores and the negatively charged electron sea balance one another and make the combination of lattice and sea electrically neutral. This structure is universally accepted today.

The concept of a sea of electrons not belonging to any particular atom is reminiscent of the resonance structures covered earlier. The valence electrons in a metal are delocalized just as they are in resonance molecules. The mobile electrons in a bar of sodium are not associated with any particular ion core, just as the electrons in the double bonds of benzene are not associated with any particular atom. To explain this phenomenon in metals, one must apply molecular orbital theory.

Each atom in a bar of sodium has the same outer $3s$ orbital containing one electron. The individual orbitals of the atoms in the bar overlap, creating a huge number of molecular orbitals. These groups of closely spaced energy states are called **energy bands**. Molecular orbitals within those bands, however, must obey the Pauli exclusion principle. So each one of this huge number of

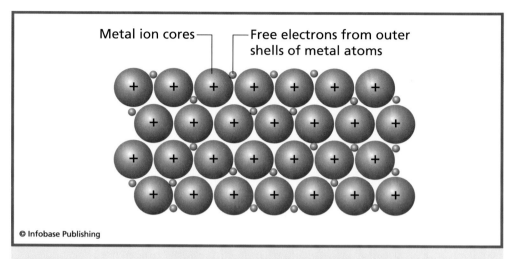

Metal ion cores — Free electrons from outer shells of metal atoms

© Infobase Publishing

Figure 6.1   In metals, regularly arranged atoms are interspersed with electrons that are also free to move. Metals are able to conduct electricity due to the flow of electrons.

orbitals can have only two electrons in it. But the filled and unfilled orbitals are very close in energy, so electrons can move easily from one orbital to another.

These free electrons give sodium and the other metals their high electrical conductivity. Pump in an electron at one end of a metal wire, and another electron from an almost identical orbital pops out at the other end. The delocalized electrons of the metallic bond ensure that little energy is required for this process, making metals highly conductive and the preferred material for power lines. It also led the renowned materials scientist Sir Alan Cottrell to propose a new definition of a metal: "Metals," he wrote in a 1960 article, "contain free electrons."

Earlier we saw that the high density of metals—much higher than that of covalently bonded compounds—suggested that their structure is a tightly packed lattice of ion cores. And the electrons that swim freely through the lattice—the other central characteristic of the metallic bond—make metals excellent conductors of electricity. But can the metallic bond account for the other properties of metals—their luster, malleability, and the photoelectric effect? The answer is yes.

How does the metallic bond give metals their characteristic luster? Do they simply reflect all the light that falls on them? The answer is no. You can prove this by putting your hand on the surface of a car on a sunshiny day. The metal is warm and on some days so hot it burns you. The metal must be absorbing some of the sunlight and turning it into heat.

The electrons in atoms and molecules ordinarily absorb light of only certain wavelengths. Those wavelengths correspond to the energy required to bump an electron into a more energetic orbital. The **chlorophyll** in a leaf, for example, absorbs red and violet light strongly. What our eyes detect is the unabsorbed sunlight, which appears green to us. The delocalized electrons in the metallic bond, however, are in bands of almost continuous energy orbitals. Electrons in those bands absorb most of the visible radiation. Some of this radiation goes to heating the metal, but the rest of it is immediately reemitted or reflected. Unlike chlorophyll, though, a metal's delocalized electrons ensure that all wavelengths in the visible spectrum are absorbed and reemitted. So, what the eye sees is the entire spectrum of visible electromagnetic radiation—the shiny, silvery-gray color of most metals. Two metals, gold and copper, add a yellow or orange tint to the typical metallic shine, indicating slight discontinuities in their energy bands.

The explanation for the photoelectric effect goes back to the alternative definition of metals as substances "that contain free electrons." Because the metallic lattice has such a weak grasp on its delocalized valence electrons, some of them can acquire enough energy from light (or from electromagnetic radiation of other wavelengths) to escape from the metal. In ionic or covalent bonds where the electrons are tightly bound in molecules, such an escape is far less likely. Thus, metals exhibit the photoelectric effect while most other substances do not.

That brings us to the last of the physical properties of metals considered here. These properties were discovered many centuries ago and have proved to be crucially important to the development of civilizations. They are malleability and ductility, the properties of metals that allow them to be beaten into shapes and drawn into wires.

One type of **bronze**, a mixture of copper and tin, was the first metal used extensively by humans. The Iron Age followed, and by the twelfth century B.C., that element was being forged into all sorts of useful devices. Most of those useful devices were weapons of war—spearheads, battle axes, and swords. Today iron and other metals are made into a much wider (and more peaceful) variety of goods. Aluminum sheathes our airplanes, copper wires carry

A Common Metallic Structure

Each atom has six other atoms touching it in each layer.

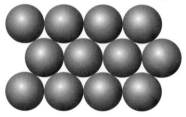

There are also three atoms touching any particular atom in the layer above and another three in the layer underneath.

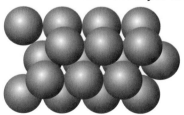

© Infobase Publishing

Figure 6.2   Atoms of metals are closely packed into a lattice configuration.

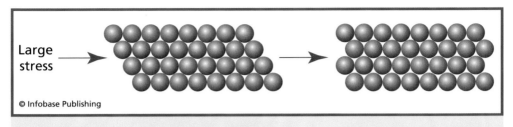

© Infobase Publishing

Figure 6.3   How metals respond to stress

our electricity, and steel (which is mostly iron) girders support our skyscrapers. The characteristic of metals that allows them to be formed into shapes or drawn into wires is a direct result of the chemical bonds that hold them together.

The lattice structure of most metals is close packed. The atoms fit together in a way that minimizes the volume they occupy. Marbles dumped into a box will assume a similar close-packed structure. In one common form of close packing, each metal atom has 12 neighbors that touch it.

Now, consider what happens when a stress is applied to such an arrangement of atoms. If the stress is big enough, the atoms will slip over one another, permanently changing the shape of the metal object but not fracturing it. A goldsmith can heat a rough nugget of gold and draw it into a wire that can be made into a wedding ring; the smith can beat it into **gold leaf** so thin one can see through it; or she or he can pour molten gold into a mold and form bars so desirable that wars have been fought over them. Remember, though, that the malleability of all metals, not just gold, is a result of the uniform lattice of ion cores created by metallic bonding.

SMELTING

Pure metals are rare in nature. Metal ores often occur as oxides or sulfides. Furthermore, those ores are almost always mixed with other compounds. One way metals can be extracted from their ores is by **smelting**. This process uses carbon (or carbon monoxide) to **reduce** a metal oxide, that is, to remove the oxygen and convert the ore into metal.

$$2CuO + C \xrightarrow{heat} 2Cu + CO_2$$

Most likely the discovery of smelting was accidental. A campfire was built over, say, an ore of lead. At the bottom of the campfire,

ICEMAN

The ages of Stone, Bronze, and Iron are well-known periods in the history of civilization. Not so well known is the Chalcolithic Age (4300–3200 B.C.). The name comes from the Greek for copper and stone, and the Chalcolithic Age is the period between the Stone and Bronze Ages when implements of both stone and copper were used side by side. This age might have remained obscure to all but a few specialists except for one remarkable discovery—the Iceman.

On September 19, 1991, two German hikers discovered a body in the mountains near the border between Italy and Austria. The body was entombed in a glacier and was so well preserved that it was first thought to be a modern corpse. But detailed analysis showed the body was not modern at all. The Iceman turned out to be a 45-year-old man who died about 5,300 years ago.

Since his discovery, the Iceman has achieved celebrity status. He is prominently displayed in an Italian museum, and investigators have poked and probed him with all the gadgetry of modern science to find out as much as possible about carbon from the partially burned wood mixed with the ore. Heat, along with the carbon from the campfire, reduced the ore and left behind a brand new substance—metallic lead, no doubt commingled with a few impurities. The low melting point of lead meant that it would melt over an open fire. It could then be **cast** into whatever form the metalsmith desired. Cast beads of lead date from as early as 6500 B.C.

Copper and iron ores, however, could not be smelted in the same way. The temperatures required are higher than those

him and his culture. But it only took a pair of trained eyes to learn that the Iceman lived during the Chalcolithic Age. The clues were found in the implements he carried with him.

Among other things, he had a flint knife, 14 bone-tipped arrows, a stone scraper—and a copper ax. Detailed pictures show the ax had a wooden handle and a dull copper blade. But

Figure 6.4   The Iceman and his tools

on this one person was a clear confirmation of the side-by-side existence of copper and stone implements. The Iceman, it seems, was the perfect, if inadvertent, publicist for the Chalcolithic Age.

reached in a campfire. Pottery kilns, which have been around since about 9000 B.C., operate at higher temperatures than open fires. Kilns may have solved the problem of smelting the ores of copper and iron. No one knows for sure, of course, but it seems possible that mankind's first metal tools and weapons came from an oven made to fire pottery. In any case, copper artifacts dating from about 6000 B.C. have been found in Turkey.

Unfortunately, copper's prime attributes, malleability and ductility, are also its biggest negatives. Copper is too soft to take and hold an edge. Thus, the earliest uses of lead and copper were likely decorative. Archeologists have found thin hammered copper plates attached to cloth, and lead beads strung on a necklace. The earliest cast copper artifact found so far is a mace head made around 5000 B.C. in Asia Minor.

Because maces can be used to bash heads, they were useful weapons at the time, but not nearly as useful as knives and swords and spears. The discovery that would make those tools and weapons possible is lost in the smoke of prehistory. Like smelting, the discovery was almost certainly accidental and happened because copper ores are usually mixed with other substances. Two prominent impurities are arsenic and tin. Some observant metalsmith must have noticed that the nature and amount of those impurities dramatically changed the properties of smelted copper.

ALLOYS

Metals benefit mankind in many ways. It was realized early on, however, that the properties of pure metals were enhanced by the addition of small amounts of other metals or nonmetals. The gold fashioned into a ring is not, in all likelihood, pure gold. It is usually a mixture of gold and copper, although the gold can be mixed with other elements as well. Adding copper to gold substantially alters the metal. Such a blend is harder, less prone to scratching and wear, and therefore desirable in jewelry. The aluminum skin of the airplanes and the steel girders mentioned earlier are likewise not made of pure aluminum or iron but consist of mixtures with small amounts of other substances added. These mixtures are called **alloys**.

Alloys are materials composed primarily of one metal, called the parent metal, doctored with smaller amounts of other metals or nonmetals. When tin or arsenic is added to copper, the metal becomes harder, stronger, and easier to cast. This metallic mixture is known as bronze, and its discovery ushered in a whole new suite of tools, weapons, armor, and decorative objects. So dramatic was the change from the copper and stone implements that preceded it, that bronze became the defining feature of the period, now known as the Bronze Age. Alloys such as bronze have played and continue to play a huge role in building the modern world.

One of the chief wonders of alloys is how a small amount of impurities can have such an exaggerated effect on the properties of the parent metal. Bronze is one example. Although there are many kinds of bronze, involving different concentrations of several elements, one common bronze alloy contains 90% copper and 10% tin. The combination of these two metals creates an alloy that is much stronger and harder than either of its components. Why should the addition of soft, weak tin to copper result in a substance stronger and harder than pure copper? The answer lies in the nature of alloys.

Thousands of alloys are commercially available today, and their structures can be quite complex. Fortunately, they can be divided into two main types. Two of the most common and widely used alloys—bronze and steel—illustrate their nature.

Mix pure molten copper with up to 11% molten tin. When the mixture cools and solidifies, the tin atoms will have replaced some of the copper atoms in the metallic-bonded lattice. This type of alloy is called a **substitutional alloy**. Some of the atoms of the parent element are replaced in the metal's lattice by atoms of the added element. Substitutional alloys occur when the elements in the alloy are about the same size. Copper has an atomic radius of

135 picometers (1 pm = 10^{-12} meters). Tin atoms are almost the same size, with an atomic radius of 145 pm. Thus, it is no surprise that bronze is a substitutional alloy.

Steel is different. Most forms of steel are made by alloying iron with carbon. High-carbon steels, which contain up to 1.7% carbon, are stronger and harder than either of their constituents, iron and carbon (in the form of coke or charcoal). This change in properties is similar to that produced by adding tin to copper, but the structure of the alloy is entirely different. Iron has an atomic radius of 140 pm, but that of carbon is only 67 pm. So small is the carbon atom in relation to iron, that it cannot replace iron in the metallic-bonded lattice. Instead, the carbon atoms slip into the interstices between the iron atoms. This type of alloy is called—not surprisingly—an **interstitial alloy**.

Both of these alloys are **solid solutions**, which occur when the constituents of the alloy are soluble in each other, like ethanol is soluble in water. Unlike ethanol and water, which are completely **miscible**, if too much tin is added to copper and too much carbon to iron, they will exceed their solubilities. The result is a **polyphase alloy**, with characteristics that are different from solid solutions. This book will skip polyphase alloys to focus on solid solutions and the important question they pose: Why are the solid solutions called bronze and carbon steel stronger and harder than their constituents?

In both types of alloys, the added element distorts the lattice but does not destroy it. Metals have **slip planes**, which under stress slide by one another. The hardness and strength of metals is related to the ease with which these planes glide by one another. The non-uniform lattice created by alloying makes it more difficult for the planes of atoms to slide across each other. Thus, more force must be applied to deform or fracture the alloy. Think of it this way: It is easier for the slip planes to slide by one another if the surfaces of the planes are uniform and smooth (as in pure metals) rather than

**Figure 6.5
Molten steel**

rough and bumpy (as in an alloy). Thus, alloys are usually harder and stronger than pure metals.

Alloys are also usually poorer conductors of electricity. The diminished electrical conductivity of an alloy compared to the parent metal is best understood by considering the wave character of a conducting electron. Electron waves, which move easily through a pure crystal, are scattered by the disordered lattice of an alloy.

Think of a still pond. Drop in a pebble and the waves flow smoothly away from the point of disturbance, spreading over the pond, as do conducting electron waves in a pure metal. Now, add a few tree stumps to the pond and drop another pebble. As before, the wave starts to flow smoothly away from the point of disturbance. But when it strikes a stump, it is scattered in many directions. The scattered flow of water caused by the addition of stumps to a pond is analogous to the scattering of electron waves when an alloying agent is added to a pure metal.

The scattering means that more energy is required to move an electron through the alloy. This reduces its electrical conductivity compared to the pure metal. Alloys also tend to melt at lower temperatures than the parent metal. The irregular crystalline structure of the alloy does not hold the atoms as tightly as the homogeneous lattices of the pure metal, thus reducing the alloy's melting point. Adding 5% tin to copper decreases its electrical conductivity by more than 80%. And adding less than 1% carbon reduces the melting point of iron by 23°C.

Clearly, the metallic bond in pure metals is very sensitive to impurities. Even tiny amounts of a foreign substance can have a dramatic effect on the properties of a metal. The next chapter will give more examples of how sensitive the properties of some substances are to the bonds they form. It will deal with intermolecular bonds. These bonds occur not between the atoms in a molecule but between the molecules themselves. They are much weaker than the chemical bonds between atoms. Even so, they can and do have a huge impact on our lives.

Intermolecular Bonding

It should be clear that the shared electrons of the covalent bonds between the two hydrogen atoms and the oxygen atom hold a water molecule together. But what binds one molecule to another? Why do they not fly apart, with each molecule going its own way? One answer is that under certain conditions they do go their own way. Heat water to 100°C, you get steam, and the molecules do fly away from one another. And what about oxygen? Molecules of oxygen do not stick together either. They are—thankfully—distributed evenly in the air around us. So, before addressing the question of what holds water molecules together, one must understand why some substances do not hold together at all. Those substances have one thing in common: They are gases.

STATES OF MATTER

Pour water into a glass and it will stay there. Pipe steam into a glass and it will mix with the air around it and vanish. Whatever is holding solids and liquids together fails to restrain gases. The reason is simple. Molecules in gases have the same attractive forces operating on them as do those in solids and liquids. But steam is hotter than water. Consequently, the H_2O molecules in steam have sufficient kinetic energy to break away from each other. Reduce the kinetic energy of the molecules by lowering the temperature to $-183°C$, and oxygen sloshes around in a glass just like water. A single chemical compound can assume multiple forms. These forms are called the **states of matter**, and there are three of them.

- Solids are substances that have definite volume and shape.
- Liquids have a definite volume but not shape. They take the shape of their container.
- Gases have neither definite shape nor volume.

The different states of matter have nothing to do with the chemical makeup of the substance. In terms of volume and shape, water behaves like liquid oxygen, which behaves like mercury. Except for the color, a solid bar of copper looks like a solid bar of iron.

Of course, as stated earlier, matter can change form. Cool liquid water and it becomes solid ice. Heat it and it becomes a gas. None of these changes of state involve chemical reactions. Water, ice, and steam are just different states of the same substance, H_2O. Now, let us return to the question that opened this chapter and make it more specific. What holds solids and liquids together? Why do the molecules not fly apart as they do in gases?

In many solids, the atoms form lattices that are held together by electrostatic charges (as in salt) or by metallic bonds (as in iron). What about liquids? What holds water, gasoline, or dry cleaning fluid together? The answer to that question came from a scientist in the Netherlands who was trying to understand the behavior of gases. His name was Johannes Diderik van der Waals.

IDEAL GASES

The concept of a gas law goes back to the beginnings of modern chemistry. In the late seventeenth century, Robert Boyle noticed a relationship between the pressure and volume of a gas. The volume was inversely proportional to the pressure. Increase the pressure and the volume will decrease.

$$V \propto 1/P$$

The symbol $\propto$ means "proportional to."

Later chemists added temperature to the equation, and by the middle of the nineteenth century, scientists had developed the ideal gas law. An ideal gas is a hypothetical gas in which the molecules (or atoms) themselves occupy no volume and there is no attraction between molecules. The law can be written as an equation relating the volume, pressure, and temperature of such a gas.

$$PV = nRT$$

In this equation, V is the volume of the container, T is the **absolute temperature** of the gas, n is a measure of the amount of gas, and R is the gas constant.

The ideal gas equation does a serviceable job of predicting the behavior of real gases under most conditions. But at high pressures, where the molecules are forced closer and closer together, the behavior predicted by the ideal gas law begins to diverge from experimental data obtained with real gases. In the 1870s, van der Waals was trying to modify the ideal gas law to make it better fit the behavior of real gases.

Van der Waals developed a new equation, called an equation of state, that corrected some of the problems with the ideal gas law.

One of his corrections assumed that the molecules in a real gas attracted one another. In his honor, the attractive forces between molecules are now called **van der Waals forces**. And these are the intermolecular forces that hold liquids together. Keep in mind that van der Waals forces exist in gases and solids, too. But their effect is most obvious in liquids, and that is where our discussion will be focused.

DIPOLES

Van der Waals never speculated about the nature of the intermolecular forces that hold substances together. He was working in a time when many scientists did not believe in atoms or molecules, and those that did had no knowledge of their internal structure. But, by 1921, scientists had figured out the source of van der Waals forces. It was the attraction between the electric dipoles of molecules.

An electric dipole is a pair of opposite charges separated by distance. (There are also magnetic dipoles, which this book will not cover. Also omitted are substances, or aggregates of substances, with multiple poles.) In neutral molecules, the two charges are equal as well as opposite. The strength of a dipole is called its dipole moment, which is the electrical charge multiplied by the distance between the charge centers.

Dipole charge q separated by distance r

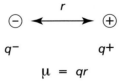

$$\mu = qr$$

In this equation, μ is the dipole moment.

What would create a dipole in a molecule? It must be, scientists reasoned, a separation of electrical charges due to an asymmetry in the probable locations of the electrons in the molecule. As was shown earlier, such a separation arises when the atoms in the molecule have substantially different electronegativities. Hydrogen chloride is a good example. In HCl, the chlorine is more electronegative than the hydrogen. This difference in electronegativity creates a dipole.

Now, consider what happens when two molecules of HCl approach each other. They will tend to align themselves so that the positive end of one molecule is near the negative end of the other. Thus, the chlorine (which carries a small negative charge) will tend to associate with the hydrogen of a neighboring molecule (which carries a small positive charge). This configuration produces an intermolecular—a van der Waals—force that holds the two molecules together. Now, extend this concept to more molecules of liquid hydrogen chloride. The intermolecular forces created by hydrogen chloride's dipole will tend to hold the molecules together.

By the way, do not confuse hydrogen chloride with hydrochloric acid, both of which have the same chemical formula, HCl. Hydrochloric acid is hydrogen chloride dissolved in water. It is a strong acid. Hydrogen chloride is a colorless gas at room temperature that becomes a liquid at −85°C.

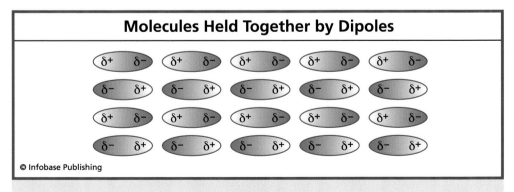

© Infobase Publishing

Figure 7.1   Molecules held together by dipoles

If hydrogen chloride is cooled to −114°C, it becomes a solid. Its lattice-like structure, shown in Figure 7.2, resembles that of an ionic lattice like those formed by sodium chloride. The resemblance, however, is superficial. The negative and positive charges at the ends of the molecules of solid hydrogen chloride are far smaller than those of an ionic bonded substance. Consequently, the electrostatic forces that hold the hydrogen chloride lattice in place are much weaker than they are in sodium chloride. Thus, the sodium chloride lattice is considerably more stable than that of hydrogen chloride. This is easily deduced from their melting points. Sodium chloride melts at a temperature that is more than 900°C higher than the temperature required to melt hydrogen chloride.

Lattice stability can be quantified by measuring the strength of the bonds in the lattice. This measure of bond strength is the bond dissociation energy. The bond dissociation energy of the polar covalent H-Cl bond is 431 kilojoules mole^{-1}. This is 130 times greater than the dipole-dipole dissociation energy of the same compound. (A **mole** is one gram molecular mass of a substance. In the case of HCl, 1 mole weighs 36.5 g.)

HYDROGEN BONDS: A VERY SPECIAL DIPOLE

Hydrogen chloride is twice as heavy as water, which has a molecular mass of 18. But water boils at 100°C, while the boiling point of hydrogen chloride is almost 200°C lower. So, why are the polar covalent molecules of water so much stickier—that is, why do they cling more tightly to one another than do molecules of hydrogen chloride? The unexpectedly high boiling point of water is due to a special type of dipole-dipole bond called a **hydrogen bond**. These bonds are stronger than other intermolecular forces. The intermolecular bond energy of hydrogen chloride, for instance, is 3.3 kJmol^{-1}, while that of the hydrogen bond in water is 19 kJ mol^{-1}, about six times larger.

Hydrogen bonding occurs because hydrogen forms an unusually strong dipole when it bonds with the highly electronegative elements of fluorine, oxygen, and nitrogen. Electronegativity alone, however, cannot account for the formation of hydrogen bonds. Strong hydrogen bonds do not form in hydrogen chloride, even though chlorine is more electronegative than nitrogen. The reason lies in the electron configurations of the atoms.

$$N: 1s^2\ 2s^2\ 2p^3$$

$$O: 1s^2\ 2s^2\ 2p^4$$

$$F: 1s^2\ 2s^2\ 2p^5$$

$$Cl: 1s^2\ 2s^2\ 2p^6\ 3s^2\ 3p^5$$

The unbonded electron pairs in the central atoms in ammonia, water, and hydrogen fluoride are all in $2p$ orbitals, giving them a high density of negative charge. Chlorine's unbonded pairs are in $3p$ orbitals. Because $3p$ is larger than $2p$, the electrons in those orbitals are more spread out. This reduces the density of the electric charge around the chlorine atom, which means it exerts less attractive force on the hydrogen atoms in nearby molecules. For this reason, molecules of hydrogen chloride are less sticky than molecules of water, and that is why hydrogen chloride boils at a much lower temperature than water.

Hydrogen bonding plays a big role in the behavior of all three of these substances—ammonia, water, and hydrogen fluoride—and in many other molecules, too. But nowhere are the effects of hydrogen bonding as pronounced as they are in water. Water, it turns out, is the perfect molecule for hydrogen bonding. Water has two hydrogen atoms and two unbonded pairs of electrons. The two hydrogen atoms are attracted to the two pairs of unbonded electrons on neighboring water molecules, one hydrogen to each unshared pair. The oxygen atom's unbonded electron pairs attract hydrogen from two adjacent molecules. Thus, each water molecule can form four bonds with its neighbors.

Keep in mind, though, that water is a liquid. Hydrogen bonds are constantly forming and breaking. So, no neat lattice can form. The effect of the strong attraction between molecules is to compact water, make it denser than similar compounds without hydrogen bonds.

Because of its strong hydrogen bonding, water exhibits some unusual properties. For example, its boiling point is much higher than one would predict, considering its relatively low molecular mass. Sulfur is just below oxygen in the periodic table, and hydrogen sulfide (H_2S) is the sulfide analog of H_2O. Even though sulfur is twice as heavy as oxygen, hydrogen sulfide boils at –60°C, 160°C lower than water. The reason, of course, is the stickiness of the water molecules due to the strong hydrogen bonds.

Another peculiarity of water is its behavior near the freezing point. Most liquids behave like benzene. Benzene is a liquid between 5.5°C and 80.1°C, not too different from water, which freezes at 0°C and boils at 100°C. As liquid benzene cools, it becomes denser. That is expected. As the thermal energy of the molecules decreases, they pack together more tightly. At the freezing point, solid benzene forms. The molecules assume the closest possible packing, resulting in a solid that is denser than the liquid. This is almost universal behavior. Of the millions and millions of compounds, water is one of the very few substances that has a solid form that is less dense than its liquid form at the melting point.

If water acted normally, like benzene, then lakes would freeze from the bottom up to become solid ice. In a benzene world, fish could not survive in colder climates, icebergs would rest at the bottom of the sea, and the Titanic might still be afloat. The world would be topsy-turvy if water behaved like benzene and most other liquids. That leads to the question: Why doesn't it?

The answer lies again with a water molecule's tendency to form hydrogen bonds with adjacent molecules. As water cools toward the freezing point, the thermal energy of the molecules decreases and its density increases, just like benzene. But at 4°C something

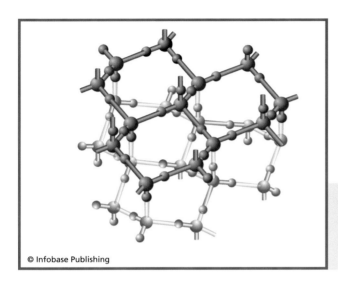

**Figure 7.2
Structure of
an ice crystal**

© Infobase Publishing

unusual happens. The density of water begins to decrease. This is because a partially ordered structure is forming in the cold water. This partial ordering becomes a highly ordered, rigid lattice in ice. Each water molecule in a crystal of ice is hydrogen bonded to four other molecules, creating the open structure shown in Figure 7.2. These molecules would pack more closely together were it not for the rigid, expanded lattice created by the hydrogen bonds between the water molecules. When the temperature rises, the ice melts, the lattice degrades, and the density of the water increases as the molecules move into the open spaces. That is why ice floats on water.

A SPECIAL HYDROGEN BOND

Hydrogen bonding occurs in many compounds. Any molecule with an O-H bond, such as the **alcohols**, will share a hydrogen with a nearby molecule and form a hydrogen bond. Molecules with an N-H bond will do the same. In fact, these hydrogen bonds play a critical role in the molecule common to all life on Earth—deoxyribonucleic acid or DNA.

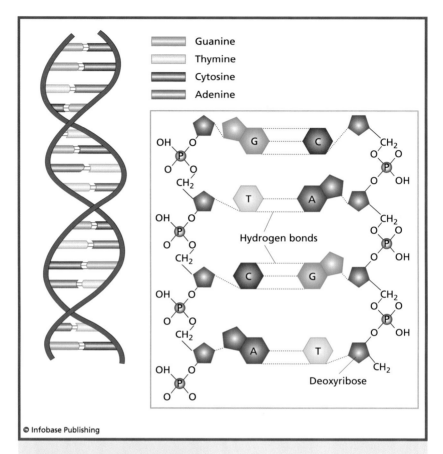

Figure 7.3   Structure of DNA

DNA is the carrier of the genetic code. Its crucial constituents are four **bases** that scientists abbreviate as A, C, G, and T. If you uncoiled all the DNA in the nucleus of a single human cell, it would form a 6-foot-long (2 meter) string upon which those four letters are repeated in various combinations about 3 billion times. The order of the letters is the genetic code.

All life starts as a single cell. In multicellular humans, copies of the DNA in that cell must eventually occupy almost every one of the billions of cells in a human body. For that to happen, the DNA in the original cell must replicate itself many times. The key to this replication is the famous double helix. When two strands of DNA—let's call them A and B—separate, each strand can assemble the other. A builds a new B, forming a fresh double helix. B does the same thing. This doubles the number of DNA molecules. This simple, effective mechanism depends on the two strands of DNA holding together under some conditions but unwinding in others. And that is where hydrogen bonds come in.

The two strands of the double helix consist of a backbone of sugars and phosphates. The bases of each strand stick out from their backbones toward the other strand as shown in Figure 7.3. That arrangement causes the bases of one strand to interact with the bases of the other strand. The bases contain highly electronegative nitrogen with hydrogen atoms attached to them. Some bases also have highly electronegative oxygen atoms.

The strongly electronegative atoms on one strand share a hydrogen with an electronegative atom on the other strand, forming a hydrogen bond. Two hydrogen bonds bind an A to a T. Three of them bind C to G. It is surprising to learn that the double helix, which Francis Crick (codiscoverer with James Watson of DNA's structure) famously labeled "the secret of life," is held together not by strong ionic or covalent bonds but by millions of the relatively weak dipole-dipole interactions called hydrogen bonds.

THE WEAKEST BOND

Polar covalent bonds are the source of dipoles. Dipole-dipole attractions, including those resulting from hydrogen bonds, hold together liquids composed of polar covalent molecules. But what about molecules with pure covalent bonds? Such molecules have no permanent dipoles. So, what intermolecular force holds them together?

Scientists realized early on that the forces between symmetrical, nonpolar molecules existed but were weak. Because they are weak, very low temperatures are required to liquify gases in which the molecules have pure covalent bonds. Hydrogen (H_2), for instance, must be cooled to $-252°C$, only $21°$ above absolute zero, before it condenses into a liquid. The question was, Why does it condense at all? What forces are acting on the nonpolar molecules of hydrogen gas that would cause them to form a liquid? It was not until the development of quantum mechanics that the question was answered.

The answer lies in the probabilistic nature of quantum mechanics. Recall that the position of electrons in an atom cannot be pinned down. Knowing this, the German-born physicist Fritz London developed the concept of what he called "dispersion" forces. These forces, now known as **London forces**, arise from fluctuations in the electron density of a molecule or atom. They are temporary—arising, reversing, and vanishing in an instant.

Sometimes, though, sheer chance produces an electron density that is not uniform. This induces a temporary dipole in the molecule. The random fluctuation in electron density that produced this dipole can reverse in an instant to produce its mirror image.

These chance-induced dipoles are temporary, but they still affect their neighbors. The small charge on a dipole will induce a small, opposite charge on the end of the molecule closest to it. The negatively charged end of a dipole will repel electrons in its neighbors,

TABLE 7.1 SIZE AND BOILING POINTS OF NOBLE GASES		
NOBLE GAS	**ATOMIC RADIUS (PICOMETERS)**	**BOILING POINT**
Helium	49	−269°C (−452°F)
Neon	51	−246°C (−411°F)
Argon	94	−186°C (−302°F)
Krypton	109	−152°C (−241°F)
Xenon	130	−108°C (−162°F)
Radon	136	−62°C (−18°F)

leaving a small positive charge; the positively charged end will attract electrons in nearby molecules. The overall effect is that a dipole induced by chance in one molecule will induce a dipole in neighboring molecules.

This positive-to-negative alignment of molecules can spread farther, creating an arrangement like the one seen in Figure 7.1. This arrangement is, of course, even more temporary than that

$$CH_3 - CH - CH_3$$
$$| $$
$$CH_3$$

$$CH_3 - CH_2 - CH_2 - CH_3$$

Butane   2-Methylpropane

found in liquids whose molecules have permanent dipoles. Not only is the kinetic energy of the molecules constantly breaking the intermolecular bonds, but normal fluctuations in electron density also disrupt the order.

The temporary bond between the two hydrogen molecules is called an induced dipole-induced dipole bond. The force between the two dipolar molecules—the London force—is, as one might guess, very weak. In helium, for instance, it is only 0.076 kJ mol^{-1}. That is only about 1/5,000 the strength of an ordinary covalent bond such as the hydrogen-chlorine bond. But without London forces, symmetrical molecules and atoms, such as hydrogen or the noble gases, would not liquify no matter how far the temperature is lowered.

One of the surprising things about induced dipole-induced dipole bonds is their dependence on size. Two organic molecules illustrate this point.

These molecules have the same number of carbon and hydrogen atoms. They have the same molecular mass and the same number of electrons. Yet butane boils at –0.5°C while 2-methylpropane boils at −11.7°C, more than 10°lower. Clearly, butane is the stickier of the two compounds. The reason lies in the nature of dipoles. A dipole is created when opposite charges are separated by some distance. Recall that the strength of a dipole is called its dipole moment, and the dipole moment is the product of the charge multiplied by the distance between the charges. Butane is the longer of the two molecules. So, the distance between the temporary

THE GECKO'S STICKY FEET

Geckos, Aristotle observed more than 2,000 years ago, can "run up and down a tree in any way, even with the head downwards." Actually, they can do far more astounding things than that. Geckos can stroll across a plaster ceiling or hang upside down from a polished glass surface using only one foot. Geckos, it seems, can stick to almost any surface, rough or smooth. To understand how they do it, one needs to know a bit more about them.

According to *The Audubon Society Field Guide to North American Reptiles & Amphibians*, geckos are lizard-like creatures with short limbs and expanded toe pads. "On the bottom of each toe pad are scales covered with a myriad of microscopic hairlike bristles. Minute suction cups on the tips of the bristles permit geckos to walk up walls and across ceilings." The suction-cup theory of how geckos can cling to almost anything stood for many years. But recent research offers a better, more surprising, explanation.

In 2002, a group of academic engineers and scientists calling themselves the Gecko Team published a paper in the *Proceedings of the National Academy of Sciences*. The title was "Evidence for van der Waals adhesion in gecko setae." Setae are the tiny hairs on a gecko's foot. A gecko can have as many as 2 million of these setae. According to the paper, the force charges on the dipole is greater. Therefore it has a larger dipole moment, greater stickiness, and a higher boiling point.

This effect becomes even more pronounced when the boiling points of the noble gases are compared. The largest noble gas, radon, boils at a temperature more than 200°C higher than helium. One reason for this difference is radon's larger size, which gives it a bigger temporary dipole moment and greater stickiness. The more

between setae and any surface the gecko chooses to climb are van der Waals forces—more specifically they are London forces, which form induced dipole-induced dipole bonds. Huge numbers of these weak bonds are required to support a gecko's weight, which is why gecko feet have those millions of setae.

Figure 7.4   A sticky-footed tokay gecko

It is often said that wave mechanics produces effects that are too small to be noticed on anything larger than atoms and molecules. The wave character of an electron can be easily detected but not the wave character of a baseball. But London forces are the result of random fluctuations in the electron density of atoms and molecules that are predicted by the wave equation. The gecko relies on those flickering shifts in electron density to astound scientists by running across a ceiling.

important reason is simply that radon has more electrons that can be unequally distributed. The intermolecular London forces are weak, but these data show how they can have a big effect on the physical properties of some elements and compounds.

SOME FINAL THOUGHTS

As Linus Pauling said, "An understanding of the electronic structure of atoms is necessary for the study of the electronic structure of molecules and the nature of the chemical bond." Pauling never said it directly, but he seemed to believe that understanding the nature of the chemical bond is the key to understanding chemistry.

With Pauling as our groundbreaking guide, this book has taken us from the strongest ionic, covalent, and metallic bonds to the weakest of the intermolecular bonds. It has gone from the secrets of ionic-bonded salt and covalent-bonded water to the surprising behavior of alloys. These substances, and thousands of others like them, have created the ingredients of modern life—taking us from Iceman to modern man. Many of these thousands of compounds are products of a worldwide chemical industry that makes everything from toy ships to spaceships, from tiny miracle pills to huge buildings, from high-tech walking shoes to automobiles and airplanes. The chemical industry is the product of many inspired chemists. It is my hope that this book will inspire a few more.

PERIODIC TABLE OF THE ELEMENTS

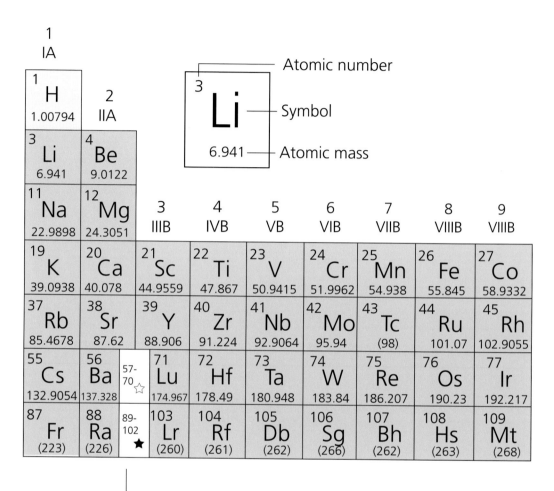

Numbers in parentheses are atomic mass numbers of most stable isotopes.

Metals			
Non-metals			
Metalloids			
Unknown			

				13 IIIA	14 IVA	15 VA	16 VIA	17 VIIA	18 VIIIA
									2 He 4.0026
				5 B 10.81	6 C 12.011	7 N 14.0067	8 O 15.9994	9 F 18.9984	10 Ne 20.1798
10 VIIIB	11 IB	12 IIB		13 Al 26.9815	14 Si 28.0855	15 P 30.9738	16 S 32.067	17 Cl 35.4528	18 Ar 39.948
28 Ni 58.6934	29 Cu 63.546	30 Zn 65.409	31 Ga 69.723	32 Ge 72.61	33 As 74.9216	34 Se 78.96	35 Br 79.904	36 Kr 83.798	
46 Pd 106.42	47 Ag 107.8682	48 Cd 112.412	49 In 114.818	50 Sn 118.711	51 Sb 121.760	52 Te 127.60	53 I 126.9045	54 Xe 131.29	
78 Pt 195.08	79 Au 196.9655	80 Hg 200.59	81 Tl 204.3833	82 Pb 207.2	83 Bi 208.9804	84 Po (209)	85 At (210)	86 Rn (222)	
110 Ds (271)	111 Rg (272)	112 Uub (277)	113 Uut (284)	114 Uuq (285)	115 Uup (288)	116 Uuh (292)	117 Uus ?	118 Uuo ?	

62 Sm 150.36	63 Eu 151.966	64 Gd 157.25	65 Tb 158.9253	66 Dy 162.500	67 Ho 164.9303	68 Er 167.26	69 Tm 168.9342	70 Yb 173.04
94 Pu (244)	95 Am 243	96 Cm (247)	97 Bk (247)	98 Cf (251)	99 Es (252)	100 Fm (257)	101 Md (258)	102 No (259)

ELECTRON CONFIGURATIONS

1 IA ns^1									
1 H $1s^1$	2 ns^2								
3 Li [He]$2s^1$	**4 Be** [He]$2s^2$								
11 Na [Ne]$3s^1$	**12 Mg** [Ne]$3s^2$	3 IIIB	4 IVB	5 VB	6 VIB	7 VIIB	8 VIIIB	9 VIIIB	
19 K [Ar]$4s^1$	**20 Ca** [Ar] $4s^2$	**21 Sc** [Ar]$4s^23d^1$	**22 Ti** [Ar]$4s^23d^2$	**23 V** [Ar]$4s^23d^3$	**24 Cr** [Ar]$4s^13d^5$	**25 Mn** [Ar]$4s^23d^5$	**26 Fe** [Ar]$4s^23d^6$	**27 Co** [Ar]$4s^23d^7$	
37 Rb [Kr]$5s^1$	**38 Sr** [Kr]$5s^2$	**39 Y** [Kr]$5s^24d^1$	**40 Zr** [Kr]$5s^24d^2$	**41 Nb** [Kr]$5s^14d^4$	**42 Mo** [Kr]$5s^14d^5$	**43 Tc** [Kr]$5s^14d^6$	**44 Ru** [Kr]$5s^14d^7$	**45 Rh** [Kr]$5s^14d^8$	
55 Cs [Xe]$6s^1$	**56 Ba** [Xe]$6s^2$	57-70 ☆	**71 Lu** [Xe]$6s^24f^{14}5d^1$	**72 Hf** [Xe]$4f^{14}6s^25d^2$	**73 Ta** [Xe]$6s^25d^3$	**74 W** [Xe]$6s^25d^4$	**75 Re** [Xe]$6s^25d^5$	**76 Os** [Xe]$6s^25d^6$	**77 Ir** [Xe]$6s^25d^7$
87 Fr [Rn]$7s^1$	**88 Ra** [Rn]$7s^2$	89-102 ★	**103 Lr** [Rn]$7s^25f^{14}6d^1$	**104 Rf** [Rn]$7s^26d^2$	**105 Db** [Rn]$7s^26d^3$	**106 Sg** [Rn]$7s^26d^4$	**107 Bh** [Rn]$7s^26d^5$	**108 Hs** [Rn]$7s^26d^6$	**109 Mt** [Rn]$7s^26d^7$

Legend:
- Atomic number
- **3 Li** [He] $2s^1$ — Symbol — Electron configuration

☆ Lanthanoids

57 La [Xe]$6s^25d^1$	**58 Ce** [Xe]$6s^24f^15d^1$	**59 Pr** [Xe]$6s^24f^35d^0$	**60 Nd** [Xe]$6s^24f^45d^0$	**61 Pm** [Xe]$6s^24f^55d^0$

★ Actinoids

89 Ac [Rn]$7s^26d^1$	**90 Th** [Rn]$7s^25f^06d^2$	**91 Pa** [Rn]$7s^25f^26d^1$	**92 U** [Rn]$7s^25f^36d^1$	**93 Np** [Rn]$7s^25f^46d^1$

Periodic table (partial)

			13 IIIA ns^2np^1	14 IVA ns^2np^2	15 VA ns^2np^3	16 VIA ns^2np^4	17 VIIA ns^2np^5	18 VIIIA ns^2np^6
								2 He $1s^2$
			5 B [He]$2s^22p^1$	6 C [He]$2s^22p^2$	7 N [He]$2s^22p^3$	8 O [He]$2s^22p^4$	9 F [He]$2s^22p^5$	10 Ne [He]$2s^22p^6$
10 VIIIB	11 IB	12 IIB	13 Al [Ne]$3s^23p^1$	14 Si [Ne]$3s^23p^2$	15 P [Ne]$3s^23p^3$	16 S [Ne]$3s^23p^4$	17 Cl [Ne]$3s^23p^5$	18 Ar [Ne]$3s^23p^6$
28 Ni [Ar]$4s^23d^8$	29 Cu [Ar]$4s^13d^{10}$	30 Zn [Ar]$4s^23d^{10}$	31 Ga [Ar]$4s^24p^1$	32 Ge [Ar]$4s^24p^2$	33 As [Ar]$4s^24p^3$	34 Se [Ar]$4s^24p^4$	35 Br [Ar]$4s^24p^5$	36 Kr [Ar]$4s^24p^6$
46 Pd [Kr]$4d^{10}$	47 Ag [Kr]$5s^14d^{10}$	48 Cd [Kr]$5s^24d^{10}$	49 In [Kr]$5s^25p^1$	50 Sn [Kr]$5s^25p^2$	51 Sb [Kr]$5s^25p^3$	52 Te [Kr]$5s^25p^4$	53 I [Kr]$5s^25p^5$	54 Xe [Kr]$5s^25p^6$
78 Pt [Xe]$6s^15d^9$	79 Au [Xe]$6s^15d^{10}$	80 Hg [Xe]$6s^25d^{10}$	81 Tl [Xe]$6s^26p^1$	82 Pb [Xe]$6s^26p^2$	83 Bi [Xe]$6s^26p^3$	84 Po [Xe]$6s^26p^4$	85 At [Xe]$6s^26p^5$	86 Rn [Xe]$6s^26p^6$
110 Ds [Rn]$7s^16d^9$	111 Rg [Rn]$7s^16d^{10}$	112 Uub [Rn]$7s^26d^{10}$	113 Uut ?	114 Uuq ?	115 Uup ?	116 Uuh ?	117 Uus ?	118 Uuo ?

62 Sm [Xe] $6s^24f^65d^0$	63 Eu [Xe] $6s^24f^75d^0$	64 Gd [Xe] $6s^24f^75d^1$	65 Tb [Xe] $6s^24f^95d^0$	66 Dy [Xe] $6s^24f^{10}5d^0$	67 Ho [Xe] $6s^24f^{11}5d^0$	68 Er [Xe] $6s^24f^{12}5d^0$	69 Tm [Xe] $6s^24f^{13}5d^0$	70 Yb [Xe] $6s^24f^{14}5d^0$
94 Pu [Rn] $7s^25f^66d^0$	95 Am [Rn] $7s^25f^76d^0$	96 Cm [Rn] $7s^25f^76d^1$	97 Bk [Rn] $7s^25f^96d^0$	98 Cf [Rn] $7s^25f^{10}6d^0$	99 Es [Rn] $7s^25f^{11}6d^0$	100 Fm [Rn] $7s^25f^{12}6d^0$	101 Md [Rn] $7s^25f^{13}6d^0$	102 No [Rn] $7s^25f^{14}6d^1$

TABLE OF ATOMIC MASSES

ELEMENT	SYMBOL	ATOMIC NUMBER	ATOMIC MASS	ELEMENT	SYMBOL	ATOMIC NUMBER	ATOMIC MASS
Actinium	Ac	89	(227)	Francium	Fr	87	(223)
Aluminum	Al	13	26.9815	Gadolinium	Gd	64	157.25
Americium	Am	95	243	Gallium	Ga	31	69.723
Antimony	Sb	51	121.76	Germanium	Ge	32	72.61
Argon	Ar	18	39.948	Gold	Au	79	196.9655
Arsenic	As	33	74.9216	Hafnium	Hf	72	178.49
Astatine	At	85	(210)	Hassium	Hs	108	(263)
Barium	Ba	56	137.328	Helium	He	2	4.0026
Berkelium	Bk	97	(247)	Holmium	Ho	67	164.9303
Beryllium	Be	4	9.0122	Hydrogen	H	1	1.00794
Bismuth	Bi	83	208.9804	Indium	In	49	114.818
Bohrium	Bh	107	(262)	Iodine	I	53	126.9045
Boron	B	5	10.81	Iridium	Ir	77	192.217
Bromine	Br	35	79.904	Iron	Fe	26	55.845
Cadmium	Cd	48	112.412	Krypton	Kr	36	83.798
Calcium	Ca	20	40.078	Lanthanum	La	57	138.9055
Californium	Cf	98	(251)	Lawrencium	Lr	103	(260)
Carbon	C	6	12.011	Lead	Pb	82	207.2
Cerium	Ce	58	140.115	Lithium	Li	3	6.941
Cesium	Cs	55	132.9054	Lutetium	Lu	71	174.967
Chlorine	Cl	17	35.4528	Magnesium	Mg	12	24.3051
Chromium	Cr	24	51.9962	Manganese	Mn	25	54.938
Cobalt	Co	27	58.9332	Meitnerium	Mt	109	(268)
Copper	Cu	29	63.546	Mendelevium	Md	101	(258)
Curium	Cm	96	(247)	Mercury	Hg	80	200.59
Darmstadtium	Ds	110	(271)	Molybdenum	Mo	42	95.94
Dubnium	Db	105	(262)	Neodymium	Nd	60	144.24
Dysprosium	Dy	66	162.5	Neon	Ne	10	20.1798
Einsteinium	Es	99	(252)	Neptunium	Np	93	(237)
Erbium	Er	68	167.26	Nickel	Ni	28	58.6934
Europium	Eu	63	151.966	Niobium	Nb	41	92.9064
Fermium	Fm	100	(257)	Nitrogen	N	7	14.0067
Fluorine	F	9	18.9984	Nobelium	No	102	(259)

ELEMENT	SYMBOL	ATOMIC NUMBER	ATOMIC MASS	ELEMENT	SYMBOL	ATOMIC NUMBER	ATOMIC MASS
Osmium	Os	76	190.23	Silicon	Si	14	28.0855
Oxygen	O	8	15.9994	Silver	Ag	47	107.8682
Palladium	Pd	46	106.42	Sodium	Na	11	22.9898
Phosphorus	P	15	30.9738	Strontium	Sr	38	87.62
Platinum	Pt	78	195.08	Sulfur	S	16	32.067
Plutonium	Pu	94	(244)	Tantalum	Ta	73	180.948
Polonium	Po	84	(209)	Technetium	Tc	43	(98)
Potassium	K	19	39.0938	Tellurium	Te	52	127.6
Praseodymium	Pr	59	140.908	Terbium	Tb	65	158.9253
Promethium	Pm	61	(145)	Thallium	Tl	81	204.3833
Protactinium	Pa	91	231.036	Thorium	Th	90	232.0381
Radium	Ra	88	(226)	Thulium	Tm	69	168.9342
Radon	Rn	86	(222)	Tin	Sn	50	118.711
Rhenium	Re	75	186.207	Titanium	Ti	22	47.867
Rhodium	Rh	45	102.9055	Tungsten	W	74	183.84
Roentgenium	Rg	111	(272)	Ununbium	Uub	112	(277)
Rubidium	Rb	37	85.4678	Uranium	U	92	238.0289
Ruthenium	Ru	44	101.07	Vanadium	V	23	50.9415
Rutherfordium	Rf	104	(261)	Xenon	Xe	54	131.29
Samarium	Sm	62	150.36	Ytterbium	Yb	70	173.04
Scandium	Sc	21	44.9559	Yttrium	Y	39	88.906
Seaborgium	Sg	106	(266)	Zinc	Zn	30	65.409
Selenium	Se	34	78.96	Zirconium	Zr	40	91.224

GLOSSARY

Absolute temperature   The lowest possible temperature is absolute 0, which is –273° C. The absolute temperature scale starts there. The unit of measurement is the kelvin (K).

Alcohols   A family of organic compounds that have an OH group attached to a carbon atom. A common alcohol is ethanol, CH_3CH_2OH.

Alkali metals   The very reactive metals found in Group 1 of the periodic table.

Alkaline earth metals   Those elements found in Group 2 of the periodic table.

Alloys   A blend of two or more metals (such as bronze) or a mixture of one or more metals and one or more nonmetals (such as high-carbon steel).

Alpha particles   Helium nuclei composed of two protons and two neutrons that are emitted in radioactive decay.

Angular momentum   A measure of the magnitude of rotational motion.

Angular momentum quantum number   This quantum number governs the angular momentum of the electrons in an atom and determines the shape of its orbitals.

Anion   An ion bearing a negative charge.

Anode   The positively charged electrode in an electrolytic system.

Aromatic compound   Compounds derived from benzene.

Atomic mass   The at-rest mass of an atom. It is usually measured in atomic mass units or amu, which is defined as exactly one-twelfth the mass of an atom of carbon-12, the isotope of carbon with six protons and six neutrons in its nucleus. One amu is equal to approximately 1.66×10^{-24} grams.

Atomic number   The number of protons in an atom.

Atomic orbital   A subdivision of an energy shell or subshell where there is a high probability of finding an electron. An orbital can contain a maximum of two electrons.

Atom   The smallest amount of an element that exhibits the element's properties.

Aufbau principle   The principle that states that the lowest-energy orbitals fill first when electrons are added to successive elements in the periodic table.

Base   A proton acceptor.

Beta particles   Energetic electrons emitted in radioactive decay.

Big bang theory   The theory that the universe began about 14 billion years ago in an expansion from a minute, but enormously dense and hot, body.

Bond dissociation energy   The energy required to break a bond. The usual units are kilojoules mol^{-1}.

Bronze   An alloy of copper that contains some tin or arsenic or other combinations of elements.

Brownian motion   The chaotic movement of microscopic particles suspended in a fluid.

Cast   To pour a liquid into a mold and allow it to harden.

Catalyst   A compound that changes the rate of a chemical reaction without being changed itself.

Cathode   The negatively charged electrode in an electrolytic system.

Cation   A positively charged ion that migrates naturally to a cathode.

Chemical bond   The attractive force that binds atoms together in a compound.

Chemical reaction   A process that creates a chemical change.

Chlorophyll   A family of green pigments found in plant leaves that absorb sunlight, beginning the process of photosynthesis in which sugars are made from carbon dioxide and water.

Compound   A substance composed of two or more elements joined by chemical bonds.

Coordinate covalent bond   The type of bond formed between two atoms when one atom furnishes both electrons in a shared pair.

Cosmic microwave background radiation   The uniform background radiation in the microwave region of the spectrum that is observed in all directions in the sky. Its discovery added credence to the big bang model of the universe.

Covalent bonds   Bonds between atoms formed by sharing two or more valence electrons.

DNA   (Deoxyribonucleic acid) The long, double-stranded molecule found in the cells of all living things that carries the genetic code for that organism.

Double bond   A covalent bond formed when four electrons are shared between two atoms.

Electric dipole   A molecule with two regions of opposite charge.

Electrical insulator   A poor conductor of electricity.

Electromagnetic radiation   Waves of pure energy—from low-frequency radio waves to high-energy gamma rays, with light waves in between—that propagate through a vacuum at 3×10^8m sec^{-1}.

Electron   A negatively charged particle found outside the nucleus of an atom. Free electrons are called beta particles.

Electron delocalization   A condition in which electrons in a molecule are not associated with any particular bond or atom.

Electronegativity   A measure of the attracting power of an atom in a chemical bond for electrons.

Element   A substance that cannot be split into simpler substances by chemical means.

Emission spectroscopy   The branch of science that deals with exciting atoms or molecules and measuring the wavelength of the emitted electromagnetic radiation.

Energy band   A range of energies electrons can have in metals and other solids.

Enzyme   A protein that catalyzes chemical reactions.

Fermentation   Biochemical reactions occurring in certain microorganisms, commonly used to produce alcohol and carbon dioxide for products such as wine or baked goods.

Free energy   A measure of a system's ability to do work. Changes in free energy can be used to predict whether reations will proceed spontaneously.

Gold leaf   Gold that is beaten into extremely thin sheets for decorations.

Ground state   The lowest stable energy state of a system. The term is usually applied to atoms and molecules.

Halide   A compound composed of a halogen and another element.

Halogens   The elements fluorine, chlorine, bromine, iodine, and astatine, which make up Group 17 of the periodic table.

Hund's rule   Atoms in a higher total spin state are more stable than those in a lower spin state. When electrons are added to successive elements to form the periodic table, they fill different orbitals before pairing up.

Hybridized orbitals   The combination of two more atomic orbitals to form a set of new orbitals.

Hydrogen bond   A weak bond between the hydrogen in a polar covalent bond and a neighboring molecule with a highly electronegative atom.

Interference pattern The pattern generated when two or more waves interact with one another.

Interstitial alloy An alloy in which the atoms of the alloying agent(s) are so small that they cannot replace the parent metal in a metallic-bonded lattice. Instead, the agent fits into the interstices of the lattice.

Ion An atom that carries an electric charge due to the addition or removal of electrons.

Ion core An atomic nucleus in a metallic-bonded lattice surrounded by all but one or two of its electrons. The ion core's mobile electrons are part of the electron sea found in metals and alloys.

Ionic bond The bond between ions due to their opposite electrical charges.

Ionization energy The energy required to remove an electron from an atom or ion in the gaseous state.

Isotopes Atoms with the same number of protons and electrons but with a different number of neutrons in the nucleus. Isotopes of an element act the same chemically but differ in mass.

Joule The International System of Units (SI) unit of work.

Kinetic energy The energy of motion. The classical equation for the kinetic energy of a body is $mv^2/2$, where m is the mass of the body and v is its velocity.

Lewis dot structures These structures use dots to represent the valance electrons of an atom either standing alone or in a molecule.

Linear combination of atomic orbitals (LCAO theory) A method for combining atomic orbitals to approximately compute molecular orbitals.

London forces   The force between dipoles created by fluctuations in the electron density of a molecule or atom and the dipoles induced by them in neighboring atoms or molecules.

Magnetic quantum number   The third solution to Schrödinger's wave equation produces the magnetic quantum number. It specifies how the s, p, d, and f orbitals are oriented in space.

Mass   A measure of the quantity of matter. On Earth, weight is used to indicate the mass of an object.

Metallic bond   The bonding present in metallic crystals composed of a lattice of positively charged atoms in a sea of delocalized electrons.

Metalloids   An element with properties similar to both metals and nonmetals.

Metals   A class of elements known by its properties, such as malleability, ductility, and high electrical conductivity.

Miscible   A term used to specify the degree that two substances will mix with one another. Completely miscible substances such as water and ethanol will completely mix no matter the proportions.

Mole   The amount of a substance that contains 6×10^{23} atoms or molecules. The number of atoms or molecules is Avogadro's number. A mole of carbon with a molecular mass 12 would weigh 12 grams.

Molecular formula   A formula such as H_2O that shows the number and type of atoms in a molecule.

Molecular orbital   The orbitals for electrons in a molecule. Molecular orbitals are calculated by combining the wave functions of the highest-energy orbitals of the atoms in the molecule.

Molecules   Molecules are made from atoms joined by chemical bonds. They are the smallest part of a substance that retains the properties of that substance.

Neutron A subatomic particle found in the nuclei of atoms. It is electrically neutral with a mass that is slightly greater than that of a proton.

Noble gases Unreactive elements with filled outer shells of electrons.

Nonmetals Electronegative elements that are neither ductile, malleable, or good conductors of electricity.

Nuclei Plural of nucleus, the tiny core of an atom that contains the atom's protons and neutrons (except for ordinary hydrogen, which has no neutrons).

Octet rule Atoms bind with other atoms to reach an outer energy shell of eight electrons. Although this rule is an oversimplification, it is still useful.

Orders of magnitude An order of magnitude is a factor of 10. Two orders of magnitude is a factor of 100.

Oscillator Any object (such as an atom) that vibrates in a back and forth manner.

Pauli exclusion principle No two electrons in an atom can possess an identical set of quantum numbers.

Partial vapor pressure The contribution that each gas in a mixture makes to the overall pressure exerted by the gas.

Periodic table A table in which the elements are arranged by atomic number in such a way that the vertical columns produce groups of elements with similar valence electron configurations and chemical properties.

Photoelectric effect The effect produced when electromagnetic radiation knocks electrons out of a metal. Einstein used this phenomenon to show that light was quantized and came in energy packets called photons.

Photon A particle with energy but no at-rest mass. It represents a quantum of electromagnetic radiation.

Pith balls   Pith is the spongy material found in the center of the stem of most plants. Pith balls are bits of pith attached to a string for use in scientific demonstrations to show how like electrical charges can attract and repel the balls. These days, pith is usually replaced by lightweight plastics in these demonstrations.

Polar covalent bond   A bond between atoms in which the electrons are closer to one atom than to the other. This leaves a slight positive charge on one atom in the molecule and a slight negative charge on the other.

Polyphase alloy   A nonhomogeneous alloy in which the constituents are not distributed evenly as they are in a solid solution.

Principal quantum number   This quantum number specifies the main energy shells of an atom. It corresponds roughly to the distance between the nucleus and the orbital. Its symbol is n.

Proton   The positively charged subatomic particle found in the nuclei of atoms.

Quanta   The plural of quantum. It is the minimum energy required to change certain properties such as the energy of an electron in an atom.

Quantum mechanics   The modern method for predicting and understanding the behavior of the world at the atomic level. It postulates that energy is not continuous but comes in irreducible packets called quanta.

Quantum numbers   The four quantum numbers—principal, angular momentum, magnetic, and spin—represent solutions to the wave equation and govern the electron configurations of atoms.

Radioactive elements   Elements capable of emitting alpha, beta, or gamma radiation.

Reduce   A process in which a compound gains electrons or loses oxygen.

Resonance Structures   Molecules with two or more valid Lewis dot structures are said to be resonant. The actual structure is neither of the alternatives but rather a lower-energy molecule with delocalized valence electrons. Benzene with its alternating double and single bonds is an example of a resonant structure. Benzene actually has no single or double bonds. Its real structure lies somewhere between the two possibilities.

Salt   A usually crystalline compound, such as NaCl, composed of a positive metallic (or metallic-like) ion and a negative non-metallic ion.

Scientific notation   A method for expressing numbers in the form of exponents of 10, such as $10^2 = 100$, $10^3 = 1,000$, and $6,020 = 6.02 \times 10^3$.

Slip planes   Plastic deformation (or yielding) of a solid metal occurs when parallel lattice planes slip past each other. Those planes are called slip planes.

Smelting   A process that removes oxygen or sulfur from metal ores and converts the ore into a metal.

Solid solutions   Alloys whose constituents are uniformly mixed. The other basic type of alloy is the polyphase alloy in which the constituents are not homogeneous.

Spin quantum number   In an atom, every electron has a spin quantum number. Spin can have only one of two possible values, usually designated as + or –. Although originally thought of as an electron spinning on its own axis either clockwise or counterclockwise, scientists now know that there is no precise physical characteristic associated with this quantum number.

States of matter   The three states of matter are gas, liquid, and solid.

Steady state theory   The cosmological theory that the universe had no beginning. This theory has been largely replaced by the big bang theory.

Structural formula   A formula that illustrates the arrangement of the atoms in a molecule. H-O-H is an example.

Subshell   A sublevel of an electron shell; different types of sub-shells can contain different maximum numbers of electrons.

Substitutional alloy   The type of alloy that results when some of the atoms of the parent element are replaced in the atomic lattice by atoms of the added element. These alloys occur when the elements making up the alloy are about the same size.

Thermodynamics   The study of heat, energy, and the availability of energy to do work.

Torsion balance   A sensitive device that measures weak forces by assessing the amount of twist they impart to a vertical wire.

Triple bond   A covalent bond formed when six electrons are shared between two atoms.

Valence   An atom's valence is the number of electrons that it ordinarily loses, gains, or shares in forming a chemical bond.

Valence electrons   An atom's outermost electrons. These are the electrons involved in chemical bonding.

Valence shell electron-pair repulsion (VSEPR)   A procedure based on electron repulsion in molecules that enables chemists to predict the approximate bond angles.

Van der Waals forces   The intermolecular forces involved in dipole-dipole, induced dipole-induced dipole, and hydrogen bonding are known collectively as van der Waals forces.

BIBLIOGRAPHY

Behler, John L. and F. Wayne King. *The Audubon Society Field Guide to North American Reptiles and Amphibians.* New York: Alfred A. Knopf, 1979.

Branch, Gerald E.K. "Appendix" Gilbert Newton Lewis, 1875–1946." *Journal of Chemical Education* 61 (1984): 18–20.

Brewer, Jess H. "The Electrostatic Force." Available online. URL: http://musr.physics.ubc.ca/~jess/hr/skept/E_M/node2.html. Accessed on July 9, 2007.

Chem1. "Atomic electron configurations." Available online. URL: http://www.chem1.com/acad/webtext/atoms/atpt-5.html. Accessed on June 29, 2007.

Chemguide. "Intermolecular Bonding—Hydrogen Bonds." Available online. URL: http://www.chemguide.co.uk/atoms/bonding/hbond.html. Accessed on August 6, 2007.

Chemguide. "Intermolecular Bonding—van der Waals Forces." Available online. URL: http://www.chemguide.co.uk/atoms/bonding/vdw.html. Accessed on August 6, 2007.

Chemguide. "Ionic Structure." Available online. URL: http://www.chemguide.co.uk/atoms/structures/ionicstruct.html. Accessed on August 6, 2007.

Chemguide. "Metallic Structures." Available online. URL: http://www.chemguide.co.uk/atoms/structures/metals.html#top. Accessed on July 31, 2007.

Chown, Marcus. *The Magic Furnace: The Search for the Origin of Atoms.* New York: Oxford University Press, 2001.

Cline, Barbara Lovett. *Men Who Made a New Physics.* Chicago: University of Chicago Press, 1987.

Companion, Audrey L. *Chemical Bonding*, second edition. New York: McGraw-Hill, 1979.

Copper.org. "Metallurgy of Copper-Base Alloys." Available online. URL: http://www.copper.org/resources/properties/703_5/703_5.html. Accessed on July 23, 2007.

Cowen, Richard. "Fire and Metals," University of California-Davis. Available online. URL: http://www.geology.ucdavis.edu/~cowen/~gel115/115CH3.html. Accessed on July 22, 2007.

Cowen, Richard. "The Bronze Age," University of California-Davis. Available online. URL: http://www.geology.ucdavis.edu/~cowen/~gel115/115CH4.html. Accessed on July 22, 2007.

Crane Co. "Chlorine." Available online. URL: http://www.resistoflex.com/chlorine_graphs.htm. Accessed on July 2, 2007.

Doc Brown's Chemistry Clinic. "The Noble Gases." Available online. URL: http://www.wpbschoolhouse.btinternet.co.uk/page03/Noble_Gases.htm. Accessed on August 9, 2007.

Douglas, Robert M. and Harri Hemila. "Vitamin C for Preventing and Treating the Common Cold." *PLoS Medicine* 2 (6) (2005): e168. Also available online. URL: http://medicine.plosjournals.org/perlserv/?request=get-document&doi=10.1371/journal.pmed.0020168. Accessed on May 26, 2007.

Egglescliffe School. "Black Body Radiation." Available online. URL http://www.egglescliffe.org.uk/physics/astronomy/blackbody/bbody.html. Accessed on September 28, 2006.

Elder, Albert L., Ewing C. Scott, and Frank A. Kanda. *Textbook of Chemistry*, revised edition. New York: Harper & Brothers Publishers, 1948.

Encarta. "Coulomb's Torsion Balance," Available online. URL: http://encarta.msn.com/media_461532301_761566543_-1_1/Coulomb's_Torsion_Balance.html

Engineering Fundamentals. "Common Materials." Available online. URL: http://www.efunda.com/materials/common_matl/Common_Matl.cfm?MatlPhase=Solid&MatlProp=Mechanical. Accessed on July 23, 2007.

Ford, Bryan J. "Brownian Movement in Clarkia Pollen." Available online. URL http://www.brianjford.com/wbbrowna.htm. Accessed on April 25, 2007.

George Washington University, Department of Physics. "Getting a Bang out of Gamow." Available online. URL https://www.phys.gwu.edu/index.php?page=getting_a_bang_out_of_gamow. Accessed on May 7, 2007.

Gould, Edwin S. *Inorganic Reactions and Structure*. New York: Henry Holt and Company, 1955.

Gribbin, John. *In Search of Schrödinger's Cat: Quantum Physics and Reality*. New York: Bantam Books, 1984.

Gribbin, John and Mary Gribbin. *Stardust: Supernovae and Life—the Cosmic Connection*. New Haven, Conn.: Yale University Press, 2000.

Hager, Thomas. *Force of Nature: The Life of Linus Pauling*. New York: Simon & Schuster, 1995.

Halifax Regional School Board. "Electrical Conductivity of Metals, Including Some Alloys." Available online. URL: http://www.myhrsb.ca/Functions/Curriculum/eng/science/9/SupplementaryPages/MetalsElectConductivity.htm. Accessed on July 24, 2007.

Hall, Nina, ed. *The New Chemistry*. Cambridge, U.K.: Cambridge University Press, 2000.

International Union of Pure and Applied Chemistry (IUPAC). "IUPAC Periodic Table of the Elements." Available online. URL: http://www.iupac.org/reports/periodic_table/IUPAC_Periodic_Table-3Oct05.pdf. Accessed on June 21. 2007.

Key to Nonferrous. "The Electrical Conductivity of Wrought Copper and Copper Alloys." Available online. URL: http://www.key-to-nonferrous.com/default.aspx?ID=CheckArticle&NM=79. Accessed on July 24, 2007.

Kipnis, A. Ya., B.E. Yavelov, and J.S. Rowlinson. *Van der Waals and Molecular Science*. Oxford, U.K.: Clarendon Press, 1996.

Kyoto University. "Einstein on Brownian Motion." Available online URL http://www.bun.kyoto-u.ac.jp/~suchii/einsteinBM.html. Accessed on April 25, 2007.

Machine Design. "Bearings and Lubricants." Available online. URL: http://www.machinedesign.com/BDE/mechanical/bdemech6/bdemech6_9.html. Accessed on July 24, 2007.

Manning, Phillip. *Atoms, Molecules, and Compounds.* New York: Chelsea House, 2007.

Markham, Edward C. and Sherman E. Smith. *General Chemistry.* New York: Houghton Mifflin Company, 1954.

Mascetta, Joseph A. *Chemistry the Easy Way.* Hauppage, N.Y.: Barrons, 2003.

Metal Suppliers Online, "Carbon steels material property data sheet." Available on line. URL: http://www.suppliersonline.com/propertypages/1095.asp. Accessed on July 24, 2007.

Miramar College. "Intermolecular Forces." Available online. URL: http://www.miramar.sdccd.cc.ca.us/faculty/fgarces/ChemProj/Ch201_Sp2001/Margarita/IMF.htm. Accessed on August 1, 2007.

Moeller, Therald. *Inorganic Chemistry: An Advanced Textbook.* New York: John Wiley & Sons, 1952.

Moore, John T. *Chemistry for Dummies.* Hoboken, N.J.: Wiley Publishing, Inc., 2003.

Parker, Barry. *Einstein: The Passions of a Scientist.* Amherst, N.Y.: Prometheus Books, 2003.

Patterson, Elizabeth C. *John Dalton and the Atomic Theory.* Garden City, N.Y.: Anchor Books, 1970.

Pauling, Linus. *The Nature of the Chemical Bond.* Third edition. Ithaca, N.Y.: Cornell University Press.

Pauling, Linus. "G.N. Lewis and the Chemical Bond." *Journal of Chemical Education* 61 (1984) 201–203.

Princeton Community Middle School. "Metals, Nonmetals & Metalloids." Available online. URL: http://web.buddyproject.org/web017/web017/metals.html. Accessed on July 17,2007.

Proceedings of the National Academy of Sciences. "Evidence for van der Waals adhesion in gecko setae." Available online. URL: http://www.pnas.org/cgi/content/full/99/19/12252. Accessed on August 15, 2007.

Purdue University. "Intermolecular Forces." Available online. URL: http://chemed.chem.purdue.edu/genchem/topicreview/bp/intermol/intermol.html. Accessed on August 1, 2007.

Purdue University. "Molecular Orbital Theory." Available online. URL: http://chemed.chem.purdue.edu/genchem/topicreview/bp/ch8/mo.html. Accessed on July 12, 2007.

Rhodes, Richard. *The Making of the Atomic Bomb*. New York: Simon & Schuster, 1986.

Roy Mech. "Properties of Copper Alloys." Available online URL: http://www.roymech.co.uk/Useful_Tables/Matter/Copper_Alloys.html. Accessed on July 21, 2007.

Royal Society of Chemistry. "Group 18—The Noble Gases." Available online. URL: http://www.chemsoc.org/VISELEMENTS/pages/data/intro_groupviii_data.html. Accessed on August 9, 2007.

Sanderson, R.T. *Chemical Bonds and Bond Energy*. New York: Academic Press, 1971.

San Diego Amateur Winemaking Society. "Grapes." Available online. URL: http://www.sdaws.org/grapes.htm. Accessed on June 29, 2007.

San Lorenzo Valley High School. "Chemical Bonding." Available online. URL: http://boomeria.org/chemtextbook/cch12.html. Accessed on June 29, 2007.

ScienceGeek.net. "Los Alamos National Laboratory Chemistry Division, Periodic Table of the Elements." Available online.

URL: http://www.sciencegeek.net/tables/LosAlamosperiodictable Color.pdf. Accessed on November 26, 2006.

Shodor Education Foundation. "Chem Viz: Background Reading for Ionization Energy." Available online. URL: http://www. shodor.org/chemviz/ionization/students/background.html. Accessed on June 21, 2007.

Strathern, Paul. *Mendeleyev's Dream: The Quest for the Elements.* New York: St. Martin's Press, 2001.

Substech. "Solid Solutions." Available online. URL: http://www. substech.com/dokuwiki/doku.php?id=solid_solutions. Accessed on July 23, 2007.

Tabor, D. *The Hardness of Metals.* Oxford, U.K.: Oxford University Press, 1951.

Utah State University. "DNA Structure." Available online. URL: http://www.biology.usu.edu/courses/biol3200-wolf/images/ DNA%20structure.gif. Accessed on December 12, 2006.

Watson, James D. and Andrew Berry. *DNA: The Secret of Life.* New York: Alfred A. Knopf, 2003.

Wilbraham, Anthony C., Dennis D. Staley, Michael S. Matta, and Edward L. Waterman. *Chemistry.* Boston: Prentice Hall, 2005.

Zimmer, Carl. *Natural History.* July 2000.

FURTHER READING

Ball, Philip. *Life's Matrix: A Biography of Water*. New York: Farrar, Straus and Giroux, 1999.

Emsley, John. *Nature's Building Blocks: An A-Z Guide to the Elements*. Oxford: Oxford University Press, 2001.

Fowler, Brenda. *Iceman: Uncovering the Life and Times of a Prehistoric Man Found in an Alpine Glacier*. New York: Random House, 2000.

Kurlansky, Mark. *Salt: A World History*. New York: Walker and Company, 2002.

Pauling, Linus. *Vitamin C and the Common Cold*. San Francisco: W.H. Freeman, 1970.

Singh, Simon. *Big Bang: The Origin of the Universe*. New York: Fourth Estate, 2004.

Watson, James D. *The Double Helix*. New York: Atheneum, 1968.

Web Sites

British Broadcasting Company. "Death of the Iceman."

http://www.bbc.co.uk/science/horizon/2001/iceman.shtml

The BBC's program on the Iceman aired in 2002, but this Web site was create to provide additional information to those who want to know more about the archeological investigation that involves a variety of sciences. For a more in-depth look at the mystery that surrounds this mummy, the BBC has also provided links to museums and other Web sites involved with studying the Iceman.

Greek Winemakers. "On the Origins of Wine."

http://www.greekwinemakers.com/czone/history/1origins.shtml

This Web site provides a historical and archeological look into winemaking, and how the chemistry of wine has shaped ancient culture and commerce. The effect of different empires on winemaking is also explored here.

Atomic Orbitals

http://www.orbitals.com/orb/

Explaining atomic orbitals with 3D images and videos, this Web
site features a large table displaying all the different types of
orbitals, which provides an image of what an orbital is instead
of just an abstract idea.

Brownian Motion

http://www.phy.ntnu.edu.tw/ntnujava/index.php?topic=24

Brownian Motion is explained using a three-dimensional image.
This interactive site allows viewers to change the data by adding
more mass to an atom.

Gas Law Program

http://intro.chem.okstate.edu/1314F00/Laboratory/GLP.htm

Molecular Orbital Theory

http://chemed.chem.purdue.edu/genchem/topicreview/bp/ch8/
mo.html

With diagrams and practice problems, this site provides a mini-
lecture on molecular orbital theory from Purdue University's
chemical education division.

The Structure of Metals

http://chemed.chem.purdue.edu/genchem/topicreview/bp/ch13/
structure.php

Using pictures of colored spheres and diagrams, this Web site
(also made by Purdue University's chemical education division) explains what kinds of atomic structures make up certain
metals.

PHOTO CREDITS

INDEX

ABOUT THE AUTHOR

PHILLIP MANNING is the author of five other books and 150 or so magazine and newspaper articles. His most recent book, *Islands of Hope*, won the 1999 National Outdoor Book award for nature and the environment. Manning has a Ph.D. in physical chemistry from the University of North Carolina at Chapel Hill. His Web site www. scibooks.org offers a weekly list of new books about science and science book reviews.

Manning was very ably assisted in this project by Dr. Richard C. Jarnagin who taught chemistry at the University of North Carolina for many years. He mentored numerous graduate students, including the author. In assisting with this book, he caught many errors. Those that remain, however, are all mine.